CONTENTS

CALLED TO BECOME

You are called to become
A perfect creation.
No one is called to become
Who you are called to be.
It does not matter
How short or tall
Or thick-set or slow
You may be.
It does not matter
Whether you sparkle with life
Or are silent as a still pool,
Whether you sing your song aloud
Or weep alone in darkness.
It does not matter
Whether you feel loved and admired
Or unloved and alone
For you are called to become
A perfect creation.
No one's shadow
Should cloud your becoming,
No one's light
Should dispel your spark.
For the Lord delights in you,
Jealously looks upon you
And encourages with gentle joy
Every movement of the Spirit
Within you.
Unique and loved you stand,
Beautiful or stunted in your growth
But never without hope and life.
For you are called to become
A perfect creation.
This becoming may be
Gentle or harsh,
Subtle or violent,
But it never ceases,
Never pauses or hesitates,
Only *is* –
Creative force –
Calling you
Calling you to become
A perfect creation.

Edwina Gateley

CALLED TO CARE

CALLED TO CARE

Christian caring grows out of our understanding of the nature of God and our experience of receiving his love and care in our own lives. As we grow towards wholeness through our own experiences of hurt and pain and as we realise how deeply we depend on the loving support we receive from others, we are increasingly moved to reach out in friendship to those around us.

1. We believe that pastoral care is at the centre of the Church's life and ministry. It is our response of gratitude to the love and care of God for us in Christ.
   'We love because he first loved us.'

   1 John 4:19

2. We affirm the unique value of each person.
   'Which one of you, having a hundred sheep and losing one of them, does not leave the ninety-nine in the wilderness and go after the one that is lost until he finds it?'

   Luke 15:4

3. We offer ourselves in service to others.
   'So if I, your Lord and Teacher, have washed your feet, you also ought to wash one another's feet.'

   John 13:14

4. We share in a mutual ministry of caring.
   'This is my commandment: that you love one another as I have loved you.'

   John 15:12

5. We care for *all.*
   John Wesley said, 'The whole world is my parish' and, 'Go not to those who need you but to those who need you most.'

   'If you love those who love you, what credit is that to you? . . . If you do good to those who do good to you, what credit is that to you? . . . But love your enemies, do good . . . Be merciful, just as your Father is merciful.'

   Luke 6:32-36

Pastoral caring is a shared commitment. Christians are called to recognise and develop the gift which God has given them. Some people seem to have a natural gift for caring while others develop their gifts through experience and training. We need to encourage people to fulfil their caring ministry. God's gift of caring involves the ability:

to listen
to accept
to be available
to be patient
to keep confidences
to learn from one's own experiences
to be sensitive to another's pain or
    loneliness
to be non-judgemental
to be able to offer words of hope and
    encouragement in the midst of hurt and loss.

Everybody is a pastoral carer and can increase their ability to care. In using our pastoral gifts we are strengthened in our knowledge that God is with us in our attempts to care and that we are not expected to share in Christ's ministry in our own strength, but in the power of his Spirit.

O Lord God, all caring begins with you. You care so much that you came in Jesus, sharing human life in all its joys and sorrows, strengths and weaknesses, successes and failures. Help me to face life sure of his presence, to serve others in his power, and to care in his name for those who need me most. Amen.

CALLED TO CARE IN THE LOCAL CHURCH

Pastoral visiting is an important part of the Church's task. It is essential to its fellowship and vital to its caring ministry. Yet visiting can easily be neglected or just left to the minister. Some visiting is essentially the minister's responsibility, but even if the minister could do it all there would be something lacking. Class leaders, pastoral visitors and others have their part to play. A visit expresses person to person interest, friendliness and concern.

Such caring takes many forms. It is practised through hospitality, through care within house groups, through our daily contacts with people, and through our prayers for people, as well as in the structured visiting within the church community.

We all need pastoral care. Leaders and visitors themselves, ministers and ministers' wives or husbands should be within the pastoral care of the church in some way.

The following notes have been written to help and encourage visitors. They could be used in conjunction with a short training course; this could include questions, discussion, role plays and case studies so that visitors, experienced and inexperienced, might help each other. The training course included in the 'Prepared to Care' training file would be appropriate and useful. A course such as this helps visitors, both experienced and inexperienced to share together and support each other.

What follows, however, is not meant to be a complete guide to visiting. Rather it is hoped that it will encourage churches and individuals to re-examine their obligation of pastoral care and to see what more can be done. In any event it is helpful to know how we are going to approach any particular visit and various possibilities are suggested.

Every visit is an attempt to create or strengthen the bonds of love that bind the church family together. It is the attempt to turn the community into a communion. And if as we visit, or as we meet people in a variety of circumstances, we try to look for Jesus in each person and try through his grace to reflect his love in all we say, we shall be sharing in Christ's ministry in a very real way.

Dear God,
teach us to see people
with loving attention
– never to dismiss a neighbour
as a problem, a case,
a bungler, an inadequate,
a go-getter, a high-flier . . .
For a label says so much less
than the truth about someone.
So teach us to look past
the label;
give us a compassionate curiosity
about the rest of the story.

Give us the wisdom
to see when we might be judging others
or using their failings
to bolster our own self-esteem.
Teach us to listen with stillness
to the hurts that have shaped them.
And if some word of challenge is needed,
then prevent us from disabling people
with our criticism;
rather, help us to question the deeds
whilst accepting the doers,
and to see with the eyes of Christ
their potential for growth and greatness.

Kate Compston

CALLED TO CARE FOR OURSELVES

Love your neighbour as yourself (Mark 12:31)

We shall not be able to respond to others with sensitivity and understanding if we are not aware of our own needs and limitations. We are all in need of support and love and care, and we are meant to find time for our families and our friends and for opportunities for relaxation and enjoyment. In fact, we are *commanded* to love ourselves as well as to love our neighbours.

Jesus knew that he needed time away from all the demands that could have overwhelmed him. So when we are tired and recognise our limitations we can remind ourselves that he went away from the crowds to rest and to pray (Mark 6:31-32); that he enjoyed and drew strength from the company of his friends (Luke 10:38); that he allowed himself to be 'cossetted' (Matthew 26:10-13); that he too longed for support when life was agonising for him (Mark 4:37-41).

We do not always find it easy to 'love ourselves' without feeling guilty about doing so but God knows we can never be all things to all people. We are simply called by him to share with others in a mutual giving and receiving which allows for our own needs and value to be recognised and affirmed as positively as we recognise and affirm the needs and value of others.

> Loving God, make me as sensitive to my own needs as I am to the needs of others. Help me to be gentle with myself and to take good care of myself. Surround me with good friends and teach me to accept their love and care graciously and with enjoyment.
>
> Amen.

Ann Bird

* * * *

We can all walk together in hope;
celebrating that we are loved in our
brokenness,
helping each other,
growing in trust,
living in thanksgiving,
learning to forgive,
opening up to others,
welcoming them,
and striving to bring peace and hope to
our world.
 . . . We believe that Jesus has called us
together.
It is where we belong
and are called to grow and to serve.

Jean Vanier

Enter into the stillness of the dawn,
the stillness that waits
below the surface of the hour's business,
the eternal quiet welling
beneath the pounded pavement of the
    world's road.

Enter in
not to escape the trouble
but to draw living strength
to give yourself to each face, each task,
    each moment.

Enter the pool of presence.
Draw peace there, to be peace
in the garden of the given day.

Julie M. Hulme

VISITING

GENERAL GUIDANCE

1.   As visitors we all feel inadequate and uncertain at times, but remember that you are offering friendship in the name of the whole Church and be strengthened in the knowledge that God is with you in your attempts to care.

2.   We can only share what we have and are ourselves and to do so is our unique gift to each other. So – be yourself – but never forget that the more you reflect on God's love in your own prayers and worship and in your day-to-day living, the more you will reflect his love to others.

3.   In all visiting and caring try to put yourself imaginatively in the other person's position. The thoughtful, sensitive visitor is the most welcome.

4.   When you visit for the first time it is helpful if you say why you are visiting. This will not only enable the person visited to understand the reasons behind the visit, but will also allow an opportunity for them informally to consent (or not) to the arrangement. For example, you could say: 'I've come on behalf of the local Church. We like to visit everyone connected with us at least once a quarter, and I'll bring the church newsletter when I come. And if it's convenient for you I'd like to feel I can spend a short time with you then, to get to know you better – but that, of course, is entirely up to you.'

5.   As far as possible plan the most suitable time for your visit. It may sometimes be sensible to telephone and arrange a mutually convenient time. If you happen to call at an inconvenient time, suggest that you will come back later if that is acceptable.

6.   Before you go, check on the names of all the family. If anyone has been, or still is, ill, ask after them. Just as important is to note the happy occasions, the celebrations, e.g. someone's engagement, an acceptance at a university, a new job.

7.   If you are not sure how to 'break the ice', start where you believe the interests of the people you are visiting really are, for example, their children, their job, their membership of Network.

8.   If, after a while, it seems appropriate, try to lead from general conversation to some discussion of the life of the church or the Christian faith. Be prepared to say what your faith means to you, but, in this as in

all things, *be sensitive!* Keep in mind your own experience of door-to-door visitors from religious organisations. Many people are not unnaturally reticent about talking intimately to people they don't know well.

9. If you are meeting people for the first time and they have not yet attended church, tell them the date of any special service or meeting. A wives' group, a men's fellowship, or a church walk may be a good point of introduction. If possible and appropriate offer to take them or meet them. You could suggest sitting with them and could certainly introduce them to others. Your church will have a lot to offer. Share the things that are attractive.

10. Another way of extending friendship is to invite some on your list to your own home for coffee. Everyone will not be in a position to do this but, for those who can, offering a little hospitality can mean much.

VISITING REGULAR MEMBERS

Some people think that members of the Church who attend regularly do not need visiting. Not least among those holding this view are the members themselves. If this were true it would imply that these people are different from other people, with no need for friendship or mutual support. Obviously this is not so.

In visiting members we may hope to:

1. Strengthen the friendship and concern that binds together the members of a Church. This is a mutual relationship and it would be good if, after a while, visits were received as well as made.

2. Become aware of their spiritual and social needs.

3. Discuss our common faith as opportunity presents itself.

4. See whether it would be helpful to encourage a member who does not attend a class or house group to join an existing group.

If you learn that a member is moving to another area, ask for the new address and let the minister know in good time so that the membership can be transferred and the member can be welcomed in the new church.

Membership Tickets

The membership ticket may give you a reason for a visit and where necessary you could take the opportunity of reminding members of any special obligations – the Covenant Service, the Annual Church Meeting, or any other events.

Perhaps the text on the membership ticket, or the 'Short Guide to Church Membership' it includes, could provide a way in for you to mention these occasions to the person you are visiting.

VISITING LAPSED MEMBERS

A different approach may be needed in visiting those who were members but are now irregular in their attendance at worship and Holy Communion and who are not closely involved in the life of the church. It is helpful to try to find out why they no longer feel so at home within the church community. To have these questions at the back of your mind when talking to them may help you.

1. Were they ever closely attached to the church?

2. Have they any real conception of what the church is for? Do they see their membership in any different way from membership of a social club?

3. Have they any problems which require more expert help than you are able or trained to give?

4. Were they ever invited to serve in the church or neighbourhood? Perhaps too much was expected of them!

5. Be prepared to deal tactfully with any criticism of the Church. Critical remarks come from regular members as well as from those whose membership has lapsed! We often find things out far too late because we are uncomfortable in the face of such criticism. A good listener needs to allow the moans to be expressed rather than stifled.

6. Be prepared to share something of what worship and Holy Communion and the fellowship of the Church means to you.

Keep your minister informed about this kind of visit. It may need to be followed up.

VISITING ADHERENTS

In any church there are those who are not full members of the church, but who attend quite regularly, maybe support the church financially, or are committed to one of the church organisations. Indeed they are often just as faithful as many members. There are a number of reasons why people are adherents rather than members:

1. They may be members of another communion and not wish to sever their connections with their own church. In certain circumstances they can have dual membership.

2. They may have difficulty in relating to certain aspects of Christian doctrine and yet find satisfaction in worship and in work in the Church.

3. They may be glad to attend worship, yet not feel able honestly to take part in Holy Communion.

4. They may never have been asked to become members.

5. They may be afraid that membership will involve greater demands than they are prepared to meet and may not want to be committed.

Bearing these possibilities in mind, our aim, first and foremost, should be:

To offer friendship and to assure them that all are welcome in the Methodist family, members and non-members.

If opportunity arises and seems appropriate we may also want to:

1. Discuss with them, as far as opportunity allows, the beliefs and practices of our church.

2.   Assure them that members of other churches can become, by transfer, members of the Methodist Church, but this issue should not be pressed.

3.   Encourage them to enter even more fully into the life of the church, and, if appropriate, to invite them to consider the commitment of full membership.

VISITING INFANTS

1.   Within the church family there will be infants who have been baptised and those who, for various reasons, have not, but the pastoral care of the Church extends to all.

2.   When there has been a baptismal service the Church undertakes responsibility for the pastoral care of the child, so that visiting the home is not an optional extra but an obligation specifically undertaken.

3.   During such a service the parents have made similar promises on their part and need the help of the Church to fulfil them, particularly if they themselves have not previously been closely associated with its life and worship.

4.   Whoever visits needs to be aware of the stresses that are common to most young parents; for example, the strain caused by broken nights, the tiredness arising from the constant demands from young children, the financial strains with which most young couples have to cope.

5.   Little acts of thoughtfulness are important. For instance, it is a nice gesture to send or take a card from yourself or from the Church when it is the baby's birthday.

6.   Encourage the family to come to church as a family. If the lack of a crêche creates difficulties, bring the matter to the attention of the church stewards or your minister.

7.   Encourage the parents to bring the child to Junior Church by the age of three.

8.   Where the parents are not already associated with the church, tell them of any activities, like Network or house groups, or leisure activities connected with the church that may be of special interest to them. Many couples look for something they can attend together. Offering to arrange sitters to free them to attend, for example, a house group, could be very helpful.

VISITING MEMBERS OF JUNIOR CHURCH
AND YOUNG PEOPLE

1.   Visit both the child or young person and the parents.

2.   If, for example, you are visiting a child who has been absent from Junior Church, make it clear that you are visiting because the child concerned is a friend whose company is valued.

3.   Take an interest in the whole of the child's/young person's world – toys, school, friends, TV programmes, and so on – but beware of 'talking down' to the younger generation! As always in pastoral care we are engaged in a sharing process.

4.   Visiting young people in their teens can be difficult as it is often not easy to have a conversation on your own with them. In many cases it may be helpful to have a chat on the phone or arrange for them to come round for coffee. There can be no fixed rules for keeping in touch with teenagers.

5.   Keeping in touch with students away from home is a very important aspect of pastoral care. Letters from a member of the church other than one's family are usually much appreciated and show a caring Church.

VISITING THOSE WHO ARE OLDER

1.   Many older people, whether able to attend church or not, have more leisure time than others.   For some an unexpected friendly call may make their day.

2.   When we are older we enjoy looking back to earlier days, when our children were young and when we were young.   Often the visitor will be the interested, sympathetic listener.   We can also learn much from the practical wisdom of older friends.

3.   On the other hand, anyone who is kept indoors for any length of time feels cut off from the local community in spite of television and radio.   Any news about the church and neighbourhood helps to dispel the sense of loneliness and isolation.

4.   Older people are interested in the present and the future as well as the past, and talk of young people of their family or yours is often the starting point of an interesting conversation.   Tell them some of the good things the young people of the church are doing.

5.   For people who get tired of their own four walls an invitation out for a coffee or a meal, with some transport help, can lift the spirits enormously.

6.   Discover what social services, amenities or clubs there are for older people so that you can suggest anything that might be helpful for a particular individual.

7.   Sometimes practical help with housework, cooking, shopping and the garden is what is needed most, particularly for those living alone. Any help given should be complementary to statutory services, not a substitute for them.   Consistency is important.   Don't take on more than you can manage!

8.   Sometimes a need may be met from your church benevolent fund. Consult the minister.   Where possible see that all the really elderly, and particularly the housebound, receive a small gift from the church at Christmas, or flowers at Easter.

9.   Transport is often a problem for older people.   If necessary, arrange for them to be taken to church, to the shops, or for an occasional outing.

10. Remember we are all growing older! Our need for affection, for personal dignity and for acceptance by others increases rather than diminishes with the passing of the years. Try always to be sensitive to this in your visiting.

VISITING THE SICK

1. You could find yourself visiting people in any of the following circumstances:

   a) the slightly ill, who are expected to recover in a short time.

   b) the chronically disabled, who may never, as far as we are able to tell, fully recover their normal health.

   c) patients suffering from diseases new to them, and who may have to come to terms with a period of illness or an operation.

   d) the mentally ill or the mildly depressed.

   e) those who are known to be suffering from a terminal illness.

   Be guided by your knowledge of the situation.

2. Be careful about discussing the patient's illness unless he or she shows a desire to talk about it. Your first purpose is to offer sympathy and friendship. Be at ease yourself: this will best help the patient. Flowers or a small gift may help to cheer him or her up.

3. You must be able to listen, but if a patient is weak you may have to do much of the talking.

4. People who are confined to bed or to the house are prisoners in their room. You will have the opportunity of making a break in a monotonous routine and of being a contact with the outside world.

5. Do not stay either for such a short time that you give the impression that you only went out of a sense of duty, or for such a long time that you tire the patient. If you promise to go again, keep the promise; the patient will be looking forward to your visit.

6.	Sick people are sometimes frightened people. They are not always sure what is wrong with them or they may not know the full extent of their illness. They may be fretting about all sorts of things.

7.	In a serious illness people are faced, perhaps for the first time, with the stark realities of life and death. They now know, as they have never known before, what are the important and what are the passing needs and desires of life.

8.	Do not force religious conversation; but do not avoid the deep things as though you were afraid of them.	Draw on your own experience if it will be helpful but avoid talking about your own troubles.	Try to develop a sensitivity to questions unasked and needs unexpressed.

9.	Sometimes you may feel led to offer a brief prayer.	This will help the patient remember that God is present in the situation that has to be faced.	Another possibility is to leave one of the Pastoral Care prayer cards available from the Methodist Publishing House or one of the cards so easily purchased from Christian bookshops.

10.	If the illness is prolonged, arrange for other friends (perhaps members of the house group) to visit as well.	Let the patient know that he or she will be remembered in the prayers of the church community.

11.	You will find that many permanent invalids radiate cheerfulness and courage.	It will do you good just to be with them.

12.	Sometimes it may be appropriate to arrange a short meeting for prayer and worship in the home.	Tape recorded services could be used occasionally.

13.	Many who are ill would welcome Communion – arrange this with the minister on their behalf and join him to share in it if you can.

14.	Remind the minister or pastoral secretary to let you know if someone on your list is sick.

VISITING THE BEREAVED

1. Your minister will be in touch with the family and will no doubt inform you of any special need.

2. A class leader or pastoral visitor should aim to know people well enough not to feel that a visit after a bereavement could be seen as an intrusion.

3. If the bereaved person is facing bereavement alone then the visitor will want to help in any practical way that suggests itself. If the family or relatives are present, then a short visit is all that is called for initially. Listening is most important at such a time. Avoid easy comfort and religious clichés. Silent sympathy may be more helpful much of the time.

4. The time after the funeral is a time of real loneliness. Call then perhaps with flowers from the church. It will often be a strange experience for the bereaved person to come to church alone. Try to help them over this period.

5. It may be helpful to pray with the bereaved person. Prayer is a recognition of our own helplessness. But only pray if you feel it would be welcomed. Prayer should never be a formality.

6. Drop in from time to time. You will find that when you have shared a bereavement with someone a closer link will be formed between you. This is part of the meaning of sharing one another's burdens.

7. Don't be afraid to talk about the person who is dead – this is usually welcomed by the one who is bereaved. And don't avoid contact with the person recently bereaved: just 'being there' when you are needed is all important.

VISITING THOSE NEW TO THE NEIGHBOURHOOD

1.   You are visiting in order to offer a welcome to the neighbourhood and to the church in particular.

2.   If the minister has received a transfer from another Methodist Church then you will be able to be given details of the family. You will be making the first visit or following up the minister's initial visit.

3.   If you are just visiting because the people are newly arrived, offer first the welcome to the neighbourhood and then introduce yourself as representing the Methodist Church. Tell them about your church but see that you have information about the other churches and, if appropriate, pass on the details to the minister of one of the other churches.

4.   Tell them something about the life and amenities of the district. Perhaps an offer, particularly if a woman is visiting, to take them with you shopping so that they can find their way round quickly, would be a good idea.

5.   Ask them to your house for coffee or tea, preferably when they can meet one or two neighbours or church members.

6.   Invite them to your church, but don't press it if they are obviously not interested or if they belong to another denomination. If they are Methodists, tell them of other members living nearby. Offer to meet them and introduce them to other friends of similar age and interests.

7.   If there are children or young people, invite them to Junior Church and midweek activities. Tell them about other children nearby, or ask a youth club member to call if there are young people of that age.

CALLED TO CARE IN THE COMMUNITY

> Isn't this the task of each church, to be looking for
> ways in which it can care in the community, rather
> than providing cosiness for its own members? The
> church's pastoral care goes beyond the business of
> oiling the wheels institutionally or helping its
> members build bridges over temporary difficulty or
> sickness.
>
> *Frank Wright*

The arena for our ministry of caring is in the day-to-day routine of
our lives and we will want always to be aware of ways in which we can
understand and respond to what others feel and experience as we spend
time with them at work or in leisure. Pastoral caring can never be
isolated from the mission of the church or from our social responsibility
and, if loving in Christ's name means entering deeply into people's pain
and hurt, it will inevitably involve us eventually in a struggle against
injustice, greed, power-seeking or violence. We are to care for the
despairing and the rejected; for the poor and the marginalised; for those
who are alone; and for the broken in heart and spirit.

Ann Bird

For our incapacity to feel the sufferings of others, and our tendency to live comfortably with injustice,

God forgive us.

For the self-righteousness which denies guilt, and the self-interest which strangles compassion,

God forgive us.

For those who live their lives in careless unconcern, who cry, 'Peace, peace' when there is no peace,

We ask your mercy.

For our failings in community, our lack of understanding,

We ask your mercy.

For our lack of forgiveness, openness, sensitivity,

God forgive us.

For the times
when we are too rushed to care,
when we are too tired to bother,
when we don't really listen,
when we are too quick to act from
motives other than love,

God forgive us.

Pietermaritzburg Agency for
Christian Social Awareness, South Africa

Compassionate God,

Open our ears – to hear what you are saying to us through our experiences and through the people we meet.
Open our eyes – to see the needs of those around us.
Open our hands – to work for your kingdom and to offer help to those in need.
Open our lips – to share with others the good news of Jesus and to bring comfort, peace and hope to those whose hurt is deep.
Open our minds – to discover new truths about you and to learn more about the community and world in which we live.
Open our hearts – to love you and to love and welcome the people for whom we care as you have loved and cared for us.

Amen.

Some passages of Scripture offer creative opportunities to reflect on Pastoral Care. For example:

1. Luke 10: 25-27   Pastoral Care is spontaneous – practical – caring – it grows out of training – it knows when to draw on other resources.

2. Mark 2: 1-12   Pastoral Care is practical – thoughtful – persistent – it has faith for others.

3. Acts 8: 26-40   Pastoral Care is obedient to Jesus' command – is opportunist, ie. it responds to opportunities for ministry offered – it offers Jesus.

4. Acts 16: 25-34   Pastoral Care is prayerful – it calms fears – it tackles immediate situations – it inspires personal faith – it includes whole households – it rejoices as well as supports.

(These passages were first drawn together by members of the Louth Circuit.)

Christ, you are calling.
In the poor,
in the sick,
in the dying,
you are waiting for me.

Christ, you are calling.
In the hated,
in the hopeless,
in the helpless,
in the haunted,
you are waiting for me.

Christ, you are calling.
In the homeless,
in the stranger,
in the children,
in me,
you are waiting for me.

I want to follow you, Christ Jesus,
so when you call,
help me to hear your voice,
when you beckon,
help me not to look back.
In the face of the unfamiliar
strengthen my commitment
and make me fit for your kingdom.

Francis Brienan

LISTENING CAREFULLY

LISTENING CAREFULLY

In our listening ministry we offer ourselves to others so that the living Christ can be present to them. As we listen to others in an attitude of openness we communicate to them our caring and our genuine acceptance and we encourage them to feel safe so that they are able to share what they most need to say to us.

Listening is, in fact, the basic caring skill and, although it is a skill which we all possess, it is still one that needs to be developed, for 'listening' is more than 'hearing'. Listening is active. It occurs when we give our concentrated and disciplined attention to another person as we seek to hear and discover the meaning and significance of what they are saying to us.

* * * *

'Listen to the fragile feelings,' says Jim Cotter, in his book *Prayers At Night,* 'listen to the quiet sounds . . . the hidden voices . . . the deep harmonies . . . Listen . . .' Yet we live in a world where it is becoming increasingly difficult to listen to anything at all. The sound of traffic, the incessant background music bombarding us wherever we go, the radio switched on in the car, are all only a part of the cacophony of sound to which we accustom ourselves. Some of it annoys us; some of it we have learnt to ignore; some of it is a welcome distraction from allowing the problems of the day fully to impinge on our consciousness; much of it precludes us from being able to find enough 'hearing space' to listen to each other properly even on a superficial basis, let alone listening to each other in any depth.

But it is not simply noise which prevents us from listening. It is also our own reluctance to find enough quiet time to listen, because true listening nearly always demands a response on our part and, as in everything else which is intrinsically worthwhile, to respond to what we hear can be a costly undertaking. Yet as pastoral carers, listening should be one of our highest priorities. We need to listen to other people, to listen to ourselves, and, above all, to listen to God – though the lovely bonus in all this is that we shall almost certainly make the fascinating discovery that there are not the clear distinctions between these three activities that we may at first have expected.

Listening to ourselves sounds a strange activity with which to engage to begin with but it is all too easy for all of us to rush through life in such a way that we 'have the experience but miss the meaning'. We can be so concerned with what we are doing that we tend to brush aside any reflections about how we are feeling about what we are doing; how we are reacting to our circumstances and why we are reacting in such a way; how we are responding to the people and situations we meet. Jesus knew the necessity of standing back from all the activity of life. He went away on his own to pray. And during the period in the wilderness he clearly listened not only to God but to himself as well. Then, and only then, did he feel ready to go out and listen to, and be available for, others.

We too can acknowledge our feelings of 'fragility', of frailty and uncertainty as well as our own 'deep harmonies'. We need to affirm ourselves where we know we have been at one with people's feelings and circumstances and forgive ourselves for our failures in compassion and empathy as we resolve to do better next time. Then we are far more likely to be able to communicate with, and listen to, others in a genuine and discerning fashion.

There is a sentence in a passage on listening which moves me – and challenges me – every time I read it. Sister Jeanne d'Arc speaks of the way in which we need to listen to each other not just with our ears but with our heart. 'We must approach our neighbour with reverence, in a sense kneeling before them, with that listening heart which love alone can give. Only by means of this silence and transparency in us will they be able to find the light' . . . we need to 'open out our arms to them in the depths of our heart.'

I love that phrase 'opening out our arms in the depths of our heart': It goes light years beyond our understanding of particular listening 'skills', important though those are, and it involves everything that we are and everything that we strive to become. It means, moreover, that listening is not simply something passive. It is an active process in which we listen to others in an attitude of openness and genuine acceptance and that we encourage them to feel safe with us so that they are able to share what they most need to say to us. It means that we listen to them because we care about them.

In one sense, listening to the 'fragile feelings' of other people can be less threatening to us than listening to our own inner vulnerability. Yet here more than ever we need to be on our guard to make sure that we really *are* listening. For care-full listening requires of us that we empty ourselves of preconceived ideas and opinions, and that we try to be fully present to the person we are with. It is about allowing the person who is with us to say how it really is with them and to accept what they are saying without judging or interrupting or imposing our own viewpoint or experience. Of course there will be a certain amount of sharing within our conversation with others. We give of ourselves as we receive from others or there is no real communication, and I would agree with Brian Duckworth in an article in the *Epworth Review* where, reflecting on his own experience, he says, 'Orthodoxy says "keep yourself out of the conversation." Practice teaches it can be balm to one to hear from another that he has walked the same way.' Even so when we are listening as carers then our own needs do need to be subordinated as we concentrate on what is being shared with us.

Most of us, anyway, are tempted to talk too much in any pastoral situation. We cover our unsureness with words and seem to feel that by our chattering away we shall leave the person we are with 'feeling better'. One of the most pastorally caring people I know wrote to me recently and shared the experience of having for many months visited an elderly woman whom everyone referred to as complaining and difficult. Members of the church did their best to cheer her up and tell her all the latest gossip when they visited but it wasn't until my friend recognised that perhaps this was the wrong approach that the person's real need was revealed. For the first time in many visits, he said, he didn't try to make her feel better. He allowed her instead to express her bitterness and anger and loneliness and her overwhelming need to be loved. It can't have been a comfortable experience to listen to so much pain, emotional deprivation and frustration. It would have been so much easier to pass the time in trivialities and comforting words but by giving the person he was visiting the space to be honest and to share her pain he was allowing for the possibility of healing and the beginnings of a new relationship where the journey forward as friends together could really begin.

Most of us chatter to God too much as well. And yet we believe in a God who speaks. He is the Word. He communicates with us because he loves us. He also longs for us to listen because loving is, at heart, communication and relationship, both speaking and listening. We will all discover our own ways of listening to God but our desire to listen may well be dependent on our vision and understanding of him. If we see him as remote or judgemental or as a 'kill-joy' we shall find it hard to hear the God revealed in Jesus. For this God who speaks to us in our caring is a God who offers understanding and forgiveness and companionship, and we shall hear him not only in the still depths of our being and in our time of prayer and worship, but also in the unexpected places. We shall hear him in the people we meet, in the stories people share, we shall find him in the problems we confront and in the freedom we seek on others' behalf. And as we do so, we shall remember Jesus' words, 'He who has ears to hear, let him hear', and know that we have begun to respond accordingly.

So listening to ourselves and listening to others and listening to God cannot be completely separated into neat and tidy compartments, for *all* listening begins and ends in God. As the God who listens, he is the one who created in each one of us the longing to listen to him, to each other and to ourselves. So if as his creatures we respond as he longs and intends we shall find that we increasingly learn to 'listen carefully' and to 'open out our arms to each other – and to God – in the depths of our hearts'.

> *Open, Lord, my inward ear,*
> *And bid my heart rejoice;*
> *Bid my quiet spirit hear*
> *Thy comfortable voice;*
> *Never in the whirlwind found,*
> *Or where earthquakes rock the place,*
> *Still and silent is the sound,*
> *The whisper of thy grace.*

> *Charles Wesley*

THE THEOLOGY OF LISTENING

1. Presence

By offering ourselves to others as listeners we can be the Body of Christ among people who hurt and have experienced loss. The very fact that we are there with them is saying – 'you matter to me', 'you are of value'. And by our presence and by our time and attention we are also conveying the feeling that there is hope in the situation. In a sense there are not even any words necessary for this to be so. Listening is a mediation of what God's presence can do for each one of us and a symbol of his love and care.

In biblical terms we can convey the presence of Jesus in a similar fashion to the way in which the pillar of fire and the ark of the covenant conveyed God's presence to the Jews of the Old Testament. And, in the light of our incarnational theology and our knowledge of the New Testament, we know that the presence of God can be communicated in and through people through the grace of Jesus and the power of the Holy Spirit if we allow ourselves to become channels of God's love as we listen to others.

2. Empathy

The word 'empathy' has a deeper meaning than the word 'sympathy'. It is not about feeling what *we* would feel in someone else's situation but about trying to feel what *they* are feeling and experiencing.

Empathy is the ability to perceive accurately the feelings of another person and the ability to communicate this understanding to him/her.

E. M. Kalisch

* * * *

You never really understand a person until you consider things from his point of view . . . until you climb into his skin and walk around in it.

Harper Lee

Imagine a person who has fallen into a ditch.

The sympathetic helper goes and lies in the ditch with him and bewails the situation with him.

The unsympathetic helper stands on the bank and shouts to the victim, 'Come on, get yourself out of that ditch!'

The empathetic helper climbs down to the victim but keeps one foot on the bank, thus being able to help the victim out of the trouble on to firm ground again.

Verena Tschudin

A helpful image for understanding empathy is to think of a picture frame in which the picture is the person's world at that particular moment. Empathy is trying to get inside the other person's 'frame'. Of course we cannot achieve this totally because we are in our own 'frame' but we can try sensitively to become a part of their world whilst at the same time keeping a 'foot on the outside'. That 'outside foot' is essential if we are to avoid becoming drawn so entirely into their situation and so involved that we become less helpful to them.

We can have no better example of empathy than the Incarnation. Jesus himself entered our 'frame' and from boyhood to death experienced our humanity with all its pain of injustice, rejection and desolation. Yet through it all he always retained his dependence on his Father beyond the human frame, from whom he drew his strength and of whose love and care he was certain.

3. Total Acceptance

Accepting people totally is an act of love in itself and it is not always easy to put our own standards and judgemental attitudes aside in order to do so. Yet it is essential that we allow the other person to feel 'OK' with us whatever their circumstances or experience.

Most people struggle a great deal with guilt so if we reinforce that feeling of guilt by our judgemental response we are being the opposite of supportive and caring. We need instead to keep in the forefront of our minds the numerous occasions in the Gospel stories when Jesus' response to those who were crippled with guilt was one of forgiveness, so that our own response to other people mediates God's forgiveness and acceptance. Our task is to do the listening and the accepting and then to be supportive as the other person works through their feelings and their problems for themselves; it is *not* to sit in judgement on them.

Acceptance of the person, while not necessarily agreeing with what they think, say or do, is what helps a person most of all to decide to change. A clear example of this in the life of Jesus is his relationship with Zacchaeus.

4. Silence

We need to give people time and space when they are sharing difficulties and hurts with us which are of great importance to them. Attentive silence is one of the most helpful responses when someone is searching for the right words or is trying to think through an issue or recall a situation. We so often try to break a silence because of our own anxieties or because we are wondering what we are going to say when the other person stops speaking. If we are not careful and if we are not able to cope with silences we may well make some very unhelpful, unthinking responses. We must learn to understand and value silence and know when and how to allow it.

God's voice is so often heard in the silence as it was by Elijah in the 'still small voice' and as it is so often in our own experience.

5. Autonomy

The word 'auto' in Greek means 'I', and allowing people their autonomy is about allowing them to find their own way through their problems. In most situations, if not all, the other person is the one best qualified to deal with whatever is troubling them and in fact they are the *only* person who can deal with it in the end. We are there to stand alongside someone who is searching to find their own way through to a situation which is manageable.

This is the way in which God deals with us. He never denies us our autonomy. We have free will. We have to search and learn and take the initiative but he is always with us, loving us and caring for us, while we do so.

6. Reflective listening

The whole Bible is a mirror into God's nature and in our listening ministry we are acting as mirrors for other people.

There are various aspects of reflective listening, some of which will be touched on again, but we can never be too conscious of the fact that it is far easier to 'image' ourselves than to 'reflect' other people.

a) Never be afraid to admit it if you have missed something that you needed to hear or that you failed to understand. It is reassuring to people to know that you really do want to hear what is being said – that, in itself, can be very supportive.

For example, if you say, 'I'm not sure if I followed what you were saying when you spoke about . . .' you are helping someone to clarify their confusion. It may be that you have not heard properly because they themselves are confused.

b) Sometimes it is helpful to give a little summary of what you have heard so far. A little phrase such as, 'Just before you said this you were saying . . .' or, 'So it was when you were both on holiday together that you met Frances . . .' can help the person to hear what he or she has said. The brief summary of facts or themes can give someone an opportunity to rectify any errors in our understanding and it can also help to lift them out of a kind of 'circling' account of what has happened. One fact in the 'circle' can stop the constant 'spin', focus the speaker's attention and take the story forward again.

c) We can also reflect back dominant feelings which may or may not be stated. For example: 'It sounds as if you're feeling really upset' may be denied but you may still be right, and to make such comments can be a way of giving people permission to show how angry they are about how they are feeling.

d) We need to be very sparing in our use of questions or we can sound very intrusive. We certainly need to avoid 'why' questions as much as possible. It is amazing how judgemental they can sound! Open-ended questions are more helpful. 'I wonder if we could explore that a bit further?' is a question that opens up a situation rather than closing it down. It encourages the person to expand about how they really feel.

All these ways of listening are about helping people to look at their problems in manageable ways and about helping us to model our pastoral care on God's care for us as we see it in the Bible, particularly in the person of Jesus, and as we too experience it. The emphasis is always on 'being with' someone as God is with us:

> I will be with you as I was with Moses. I will not leave you or desert you.
>
> *Joshua 1:5*

> Even though I go through the deepest darkness . . . you are with me.
>
> *Psalm 23:4*

> Lo, I am with you always, even unto the end of the world.
>
> *Matthew 28:20*

* * * *

Jesus listened to people, heard their need and responded in a way which left the responsibility with the other person. He also offered them hope.

When we listen to those who share with us we are modelling God's care for his people. We listen and respond to people in love in the hope that they will be enabled to discover more of the fullness of life which God in his love wants for all of us.

Ann Bird

I NEED TO LISTEN

How strange it is, O Lord,
    that I should feel I need to ask you to hear me.
Is it not I who need to learn to listen?
Should I not ask you to jerk me to my feet,
    to snatch me out of my drowsy indifference,
    to nudge me into alertness?
I am constantly surrounded by sounds I do not hear,
    by voices to which I am indifferent.

This is a singing world.
There are voices of angels
    and voices of lovers
    and voices of those inviting me to gladness everywhere.
Enable me to hear them, I pray,
    and in the hearing be lifted up to gratitude
    for the mystery and magic of being human.

This is a sobbing world.
There are voices filled with echoes of hurt and pain everywhere.
There are voices almost choked out by tears
    and voices that come out of aching.
There are hollow voices, empty voices.
I would rather not hear them –
    the voices of hungry children
    and of sorrowing women
    and of desperate men.
But they are all around me.
Enable me to hear them, I pray,
    and in the hearing
    be able to identify my brothers and sisters.

This is a shouting world.
There are voices of rage and protest,
    of defiance and of contempt.
How carefully I sift out the shouting,
    ignore the screaming.
Make me listen, O God, I pray.
For you are the father of us all,
    and sometimes the voices of anger carry messages from you.
Enable me to be a listener, I ask.
For in listening I may find direction and guidance.

Help me to listen to myself –
   to still, small voices of conscience,
   to whispers of faith,
   and to the soft inner humming of hope.

Help me to learn to trust myself more than I do,
   trust myself not because I am wise and good,
   but because I am loved and wanted.

I remember how the Lord Jesus spoke of your love for me
   and went all the way to a cross to show its meaning.
Help me to listen to others –
   to the person who is trying to tell me he loves me,
   and the person who is trying to tell me
   he needs my love in return.
Help me to listen to the stranger who may be an angel in disguise,
   to the friend who may be lonely and lost.
Help me to listen to the angry and outraged
   who may be saying to me words I need to hear.

Steady me, O God, as a listener.
And when I speak, make me careful lest I use words as weapons
   and language as a severing sword.
Enable me to sort out what I hear
   and not be thrown off balance
   by the careless tongues of others.
Teach me to realise that just because a lie is spoken over and over,
   it does not become true.
Just because a falsehood is spoken loudly,
   it does not become less false.
So when prejudice and passion weight the words I hear
   with divisiveness and conflict,
   give me sense enough to reject them.
Give me judgement and common sense to cut through words
   that evade and distort lest I be misled.
Steady me, O Lord, as I learn to listen. Amen.

Kenneth G. Phifer

LISTENING AND REFLECTING

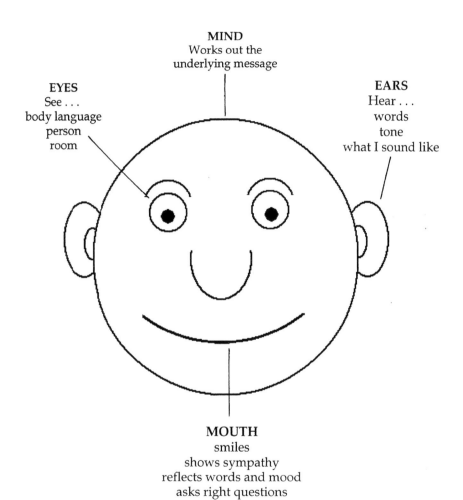

MIND
Works out the
underlying message

EYES
See . . .
body language
person
room

EARS
Hear . . .
words
tone
what I sound like

MOUTH
smiles
shows sympathy
reflects words and mood
asks right questions

Be relaxed
Don't be afraid of silence
Don't tell your life story
Watch your body language

LISTENING SKILLS – 1

"Man's real need, his most terrible need, is for someone to listen to him, not as a patient but as a human soul. He needs to tell someone of what he thinks, of the bewilderment he encounters when he tries to discover why he was born how he must live, and where his destiny lies . . . who will listen to me when my heart is breaking, when I am troubled and confused?"

Life is about relationships; we have a need within us to relate to other people. Isolation is not natural for us. When we get good news we want to share it with someone; when we are upset we need to find someone to share our burden. A person who is isolated, who has no real point of contact with other folk, is likely to be very unhappy.

Think about the traditional role of the family unit. Families lived in the same area, the same street or village. Growing-up was a shared experience, and parenthood was guided by grandparents who also took on the role of confessor and source of wisdom. The family network provided support and at its best was a safe place to be. Independence was not a priority; members of the family could share their concerns if they so wished.

Consider our society today. Independence *is* a priority. Families are fragmented as the young leave home and migrate in search of work. The elderly have become devalued. Old age is not something to be revered, but is now something to be feared. Look how society treats its elderly. Old age is socially unacceptable; our elderly are placed in homes. We now live in a generation that has cultivated privacy and isolation. Loneliness is one of the major problems of our age. Who do the lonely, the isolated, the worried and the depressed find to talk to?

The greatest gift that one human being can give to another is their undivided attention. To be a good effective listener is not easy, it requires certain skills. If a person is given an opportunity to talk about a problem, the chances are that they will find a solution for themselves. Talking enables you to lay out the concern to examine it from different angles, to put it in perspective and to deal with it. To help a person to open up and examine their concerns requires gentle leading and encouragement. This is the art of good listening.

Some dos and don'ts

Do reflect back on what you are hearing. **Do** paraphrase to show understanding. **Do** summarise to check that you have got it right. **Don't** offer your solutions. **Don't** blame or lecture. **Don't** interpret or divert the conversation. **Be** natural! Remember, as a listener you are helping someone to find the solution to their problems, you are not an expert on their life. If you offer solutions and they don't work then it's your fault! Remember the spider and his silk: by sensitive listening you can build a bridge of safety and confidence.

LISTENING SKILLS – 2

We have spoken of the need for a caring listener to allow the sufferer to control the conversation. We are sometimes scared of silence, but for some people, simply to be quiet with a person whom they trust is all that is necessary. We can help by listening to the silence. We can also listen by means of touch. Words are not the automatic solution to everyone's troubles. Jesus reached out and touched; sometimes we should offer touch as an expression of our love and concern, although we have to be extremely careful that touching is appropriate, particularly in the light of the 'Safeguarding Children & Young People' report.

Empathy is the ability to stand in the other person's shoes and feel as they do. To be a good empathetic listener we must listen without any elements of judgement or compliance. We sometimes have the difficult task of accepting the person just as they are. This is a basic Christian response; we talk about the accepting love of God who seeks out the lost. We must seek to help people to accept themselves and see for themselves the way that they can change or affect their condition. However, a person must want to change. We cannot make them! If we try to make them, then we simply become interfering 'do-gooders'. A person has a right to their own personal misery even to the point of taking action that you or I would find unacceptable. We can only offer the listening help. However, it may be rejected and that will hurt us. So be it! We do not have all the answers, and even if we believe that we do, we must keep them to ourselves.

In the listening process there are four stages along the road. We need to help the person to see for themselves:

a) My life as it is now
b) My life as I would like it to be
c) What stops me from becoming what I would like to be?
d) What am I doing, or can I do, about it?

In conversation we can explore each of these questions by listening creatively. We must try to keep all avenues open and, above all, let the sufferer steer the conversation. We can assist the process by our empathetic listening. We can kill the flow of conversation by our inappropriate responses to things we hear. We have to strive hard to be neutral. This is very difficult for the Christian, because we have so much to say about our view of suffering and death, about guilt and fear. We have our faith and our beliefs; these can be offered if appropriate but never, repeat, never, imposed! If asked about our faith we can respond with what it means to us; this may be helpful or it may not. Careful judgement must be exercised.

Things to do

Try and listen to yourself as you speak to other people. Listen for words or phrases that sound critical or judgemental, blaming or lecturing. One of the most critical sounding words in the English language is the little word, Why? Think about it.

LISTENING SKILLS – 3

The Americans, who have a word for everything, have coined the word, 'stroking'. If you own a cat and it sits on your lap and you gently stroke it, you will hear it purr with contentment. If, however, you stroke the cat the wrong way, i.e. backwards, you will make the cat feel uncomfortable and irritable and you will end up getting scratched or spat at!

This is a good illustration of the way that we treat people. We can 'stroke' them positively or negatively. It is human nature for us to like those people who are nice to us and who think as we do. The people we tend to dislike are those who perhaps dislike us or who think differently from us. It is also human nature to find fault and to criticise. Why are newspapers full of bad news rather than good? Somehow the darker side of life seems to hold a greater attraction for us. Possibly the best example of this is gossip. Gossip tends to be about the darker side of life – bad news spreads very quickly!

There is a popular poster which carries the following message:

Constantly criticise a child and he will grow up critical of others.
Constantly brutalise a child and he will grow up to brutalise others.
Tell a child that he is worthless and he will become worthless in his own eyes.
Force a child beyond his ability and he will become a failure.
Show a child that life is pointless and he will grow into an aimless adult.

Tell a person on the other hand, that she is loved and that her skills are worthwhile, that life is to be enjoyed rather than endured, bolster her strengths and support her weaknesses – then you are 'stroking' in a positive way and relationships will blossom.

When did you last tell someone that you appreciated them? Suppose we were to get together in twos and simply say to each other, 'The things that I really appreciate about you are . . .' What would it feel like?

When we 'stroke' someone in a positive way we do two things. Firstly, we encourage truth and openness. Secondly, we affirm the strengths of the other person, and we may even provide insights into their life that they have never seen before. This helps us to improve our own view of ourselves. There is a good Christian foundation for this. Jesus said, 'Love others as you love yourself.' *Do* you love yourself? Many people actually despise themselves; they are full of self-doubts, full of guilt and anxiety. These can drag a person down into a depressed state. One piece of practical theology! Jesus tells us God loves us. He doesn't wait until we become good people. He starts by loving us as we are now. He alone knows what we are capable of, but he starts with us as we are right now. If God loves us as we are, with all our faults and weaknesses, why can't we love ourselves? When we begin to accept ourselves as we are, then we start the process that we talked of before, this time listening to ourselves as we think about:

a)   My life as it is now
b)   My life as I would like it to be
c)   What stops me from becoming what I would like to be?
d)   What am I doing, or can I do, about it?

For many people, one of the most difficult subjects to talk about is death. Many folk go to great lengths to try and avoid facing up to what is the one certainty for every one of us. We will all die. A cynical comment I once heard went like this – 'From the day you are born you are terminal.' Sooner or later, within our own families and within the family of the church, we will come into contact with death and with the grief that follows. For the listener this is perhaps one of the most valuable and demanding areas of service. All the guidelines that we have talked about apply here as well. Sudden death will require expert help from a number of sources, and we as listeners may come into the situation a little later on. Fortunately most deaths are expected and follow a period of illness. Let us think about what we may call a typical situation. An elderly man has died following a long illness. He leaves behind a widow. Without wishing to make absolute rules, there are four stages that she will go through as she comes to terms with her loss. There is no set time for any of the stages. Grieving may last for weeks, or it may last for many months.

Disbelief and shock
Even though death is expected, when it happens it still comes as a great shock to those closest to the deceased. There is a numbness and a denial of what has happened. Some will throw themselves into a frenzy of activity, others will simply sit and stare. There is a lot to do: arrangements to make and people to notify, and these buoy up the widow, often to the point where people will remark, 'Isn't she taking it well!' Sometimes the widow will carry on as if nothing has happened. Soon, however, and often following the funeral, comes the emotional reaction.

The pain of grief, yearning and anger
For many, the funeral gives permission to express what has been blocked up inside. The tears come and sometimes great anger is expressed: anger towards God, anger towards themselves, anger towards the one who has died. The reality of the situation is now becoming clear. It is at this point that relatives return home and the support begins to dwindle. Regrettably we see at this stage the 'snap out of it' brigade. 'You must pull yourself together and live your own life.' This is not for the benefit of the widow, it is for the benefit of family and friends who do not know how to cope with a grief-stricken and distraught member of the family. How can you expect in a few

days to replace a husband who perhaps has lived with his wife for forty or fifty years? It is unreasonable to expect a readjustment so soon.

Despair
The feeling of never being able to cope. The feeling of being only half a person. The knowledge that folk are avoiding you because they don't know what to say. The stupid mistakes like setting the table for two, or hearing your loved one around the house. Sleeplessness, tight chest, no appetite, seeing life go on around you as if nothing had happened. Coming home to an empty house, family telling you to sell up. Business letters that arrive and you don't know what to do with them, a garden that is getting overgrown. Despair. This stage gives way to the next.

Acceptance and reorganisation
Finally acceptance comes and with it the ability to 'let go'. The widow begins to sort out her life and establish new relationships and routines. The pain of loss never fully goes. There are still anniversaries and birthdays to cope with, Christmas and special shared days that bring back the memories. Activity becomes important again; to be busy helps to fill a day which could otherwise be empty.

What can we do as good listeners?

We need to encourage bereaved folk to talk about the one who has died. We tend to shy away from this simply because it makes us feel uncomfortable and we may not be able to cope with the response. Tears are healing and, believe it or not, most folk who have lost a loved one actually want to talk to someone about them and also about how they are feeling themselves. If by listening you are able to let another express their grief, then you are doing a valuable service. As you get to know the person better you can even begin to explore not only the good things about them. As time passes it helps to recall that perhaps they were not saintly all the time. This is all part of the acceptance process. In bereavement, the four stages that we have discussed before still apply. By listening we can help the person to rebuild their life as they would like it, given their circumstances. Remember, there will be some who will never get over the death of a loved one.

Finally, as Christians we have something very positive to say about death. As we listen we will almost certainly hear the person seek assurances about the one who has died. This may be an opportunity to talk about your faith. When all else seems to be inadequate, I simply assert the truth as I see it, that, 'They are in the hands of God.' I do not get drawn into speculation about judgement or heaven and hell. These images are not always helpful. Remember that as good listeners we do not judge the one we are listening to, and it follows that we do not judge the one who has died.

Working with folk who are dying or with folk who are bereaved will bring you face to face with your own mortality and that could be disturbing. You will need to think out your own attitude towards your own death. This is not morbid, rather it is a recognition that death is a part of life and we are not exempt.

Michael Langstaff

- Pay attention to the way in which you listen to other people at home or wherever else you meet and chat.

- 'When someone is in a climate of listening they'll say things they wouldn't have said before' (Dame Cicely Saunders). What helps to create a 'climate of listening' so that people are enabled to speak freely?

- Reflect on the following words:

  a) Listening is 'the highest form of hospitality'.
  b) We need to learn to listen to ourselves before we can truly learn to listen to other people.
  c) The Church today is notoriously bad at listening and being still and quiet enough to do so.

Learn to be still in order to listen. Learn to be still in order to see. Learn to create a space at the centre of your being where you are open to the Spirit of God.

* * * *

By listening it is possible to bring a person's soul into being.

Listen to yourself, so as to find the path to God
        within the frail walls of your humanness,
Listen to yourself, for it is you alone who will lead
        yourself to him, or away from him.
Listen to yourself, listen to God, when you have led
        yourself to him.
Listen well, for if you hear his voice
you will be wise with the wisdom of the Lord,
and then you will be able to hear the voice of men,
not as a surging sea, or as a mob.
But each man's speech is his own,
a treasure given to you beyond all expectations,
because you led yourself to him and listened
        to his voice.

Catherine de Hueck Doherty

* * * *

LISTEN

When I ask you to listen to me
and you start giving advice you have
not done what I asked

When I ask you to listen to me
and you begin to tell me why I
shouldn't feel that way you are
trampling on my feelings

When I ask you to listen to me
and you feel you have to do something
to solve my problems you have failed
me, strange as that may seem

When you do something for me that I
can and need to do for myself, you
contribute to my fear and weakness

So, please listen and just hear me, and,
if you want to talk, wait a minute for
your turn: and I will listen to you.

Anonymous

THE TELEPHONE

I have just hung up, why did he telephone?
I don't know . . . Oh! I get it . . .
I talked a lot and listened very little.

Forgive me, Lord, it was a monologue and not a
dialogue.
I explained my idea and did not get his;
Since I didn't listen, I learned nothing,
Since I didn't listen, I didn't help,
Since I didn't listen, we didn't communicate.

Forgive me, Lord, for we were connected,
And now we are cut off.

Michel Quoist

* * * *

Every one of our fellow men is in search of a heart ready to listen to him in such a way that he will no longer be **another** human being. Let us then try to give this kind of welcome, to pay him that depth of attention which comes from the bottom of the heart so that he will be at ease with us as he is with himself. So often the eyes of those who surround him and even of those closest to him are like so many distorting mirrors; instead, let him find in us a heart so clear and transparent that the refraction index, so to speak, is nil. 'Bear one another's burden' (Ga. 6:2). We are so very weak that we are often unable to bear anyone else's burden. However, we can always at least relieve him of his load by letting him pour it out into us. All we have to do is to listen with our heart. It is not simply a question of exchanging confidences, though this may well come into it. It is a question of an interior welcome at a deep level, of a heart so full of fellow-feelings as to be on the alert for all that is best, and frequently most hidden and unexpressed, in all those with whom we come into contact . . . We must approach our neighbour with reverence, in a sense kneeling before him, with that listening heart which love alone can give. Only by means of this silence and transparency in us will he be able to find the light. By thus opening out our arms to him in the depths of our heart, we shall ensure that our own response offers him precisely that truth which he can assimilate.

Sister Jeanne d'Arc

Loving Jesus, give us hearts that listen. Hearts that listen to thee in silence and love. Hearts that listen to those we meet, to those in trouble, in the silence of true compassion, Thy compassion and understanding. Help us to remember that there is a time for silence and a time for speaking, and give us the wisdom to know when to speak and when to hold our peace.

Forgive us for all the times we have failed to listen and so missed the chance to help, leaving our friend uncomforted.

Silence us, compassionate God, for thy name's sake.

Amen.

Teach me to listen, Lord,
to those nearest me,
my family, my friends, my co-workers.
Help me to be aware that
no matter what words I hear,
the message is,
'Accept the person I am. Listen to me.'

Teach me to listen, Lord,
to those far from me
the plea of the forgotten,
the cry of the anguished.

Teach me to listen, Lord,
to myself.
Help me to be less afraid,
to trust the voice inside –
in the deepest part of me.

Teach me to listen, Lord,
for your voice –
in busyness and in boredom,
in certainty and doubt,
in noise and in silence.

Teach me, Lord, to listen.

John Veltri SJ

Recommended Reading and Reflection

Listening, Anne Long (Daybreak)

At the end of Anne Long's book there are listening exercises relating to each chapter. These helpful questions may be used for personal reflection and prayer or in a group context.

Still Small Voice, Michael Jacobs (New Library of Pastoral Care/SPCK)
Swift To Hear

Swift to Hear includes very useful listening exercises for use in groups.

Listening to God, Joyce Huggett (Hodder & Stoughton)

Christian Listeners Group, *Listening Pack,* The Acorn Christian Healing Trust, Whitehill Chase, Bordon, Hants.

A group resource including four group sessions and two tapes:

Session 1. Listening to God
      2. Listening to Others
      3. Listening to God for our Church
      4. Listening to God for the World

For those who wish to think more fully about caring for the bereaved there is a training course written by Jenny Pardoe included in 'Prepared to Care', the pastoral care training file. Entitled 'Grief, Bereavement and Loss' it consists of eight sessions and is excellent material for house groups or for individual reflection.

CONFIDENTIALITY

In 1993 the General Purposes Committee presented a report on Confidentiality and Pastoral Care to the Methodist Church Conference. The full report is available from the Methodist Publishing House but here are some extracts which are relevant to all pastoral ministry.

Sharing Confidences

Confidential information is shared in the normal course of friendship. It is a sign of a developing relationship that areas of experience which are not open to public gaze are revealed to a friend. The process is expected to be two-way and the mutual understanding involved will normally enable both parties to sense what is private and what may be publicly disclosed. If, however, this privacy is breached there is bound to be a feeling of betrayal.

General Principles

Life in the church and the exercise of ministry in all its forms are built upon trust. Where trust is eroded Christian fellowship ceases to be genuinely supportive and ministry fails to reach the deeper levels of need. It falls upon every member of the Christian community to develop and maintain such trust.

Happily this is often the case. It would distort the picture if we did not recognise that in countless instances people have found strength and the recovery of self-esteem because they were able to turn to someone else in the church for help in the absolute confidence that trust would not be betrayed. Nevertheless problems do arise. For a variety of reasons people can be careless in what they relay about each other and great damage is done.

In general it should be taken for granted that information given or received in confidence will be kept confidential. Unless this is so the needy will have nowhere to turn for help. When, therefore, a person indicates that what he or she is saying is to be kept confidential, it should be understood without question that it will remain so.

Suggested guidelines

a) Be sensitive; use your imagination. Put yourself in the other person's shoes. Recall what you know of their circumstances. In their place, would you want this bit of information more widely known? If not widely known, would you object to particular persons knowing?

b) Recall the instant when the information was given. What clues did the speaker give? Hesitation? Embarrassment? Pleasure? Was it in character for them to talk about themselves in this way?

c) What is your own reaction to the news? If you have an urge to tell, ask yourself why. Beware especially if you are shocked, alarmed or offended.

d) Wherever possible ask permission before sharing confidential information with someone else, and explain why you think it would be helpful to do so.

e) Beware of situations where other people appear to know what you know, but in fact may know less, or be fishing for more.

f) Make no assumptions. What a person has told you may not be known to other members of his or her family, and he or she may not wish it to be.

g) Beware of careless talk at the breakfast table. If a matter is not to be divulged, it may not be spoken of at home, not least in the manse. A spouse or children should not be made to shoulder such responsibility. They should be helped to understand why you cannot share such things with them.

Shared Support

('What about the prayer group?')

The caring ministries of the church, and in particular its ministry of prayer, depend on the sharing of knowledge. Unless needs are known appropriate support cannot be offered. But information passed on out of loving concern to those who are committed to help can easily degenerate into gossip, running freely and from less worthy motives.

Many people would welcome the thought that others were praying for them in a time of trouble or knew of their problem and were willing to help. At the same time they might well not want their difficulties known all over the church or the neighbourhood. What principles should be observed here?

Suggested guidelines

a) Ask permission first and explain why you are seeking it. Identify the group with whom you will share the knowledge.

b) Make it clear to those whom you tell what limits are placed on the information. They must agree to abide by those limits if they are to continue to be treated as members of the caring group.

c) Avoid being over-dramatic. Talk of 'secrets' increases the pulse-rate and tempts people to feel important. This makes silence harder to keep.

Deliberate revelations

('Did you hear what I heard? . . .')

Sometimes a sense of self-importance impels people to let it be known that they possess information not shared by others. They easily allow themselves to be drawn from hinting that they possess such knowledge into revealing what it is. Occasionally, though we hope rarely, confidentiality may be breached out of anger or malice.

> ### Suggested guidelines
>
> What guidelines can be offered here, except, by the grace of God, to know oneself better, to keep a watch on one's motives, and to put the love of one's neighbour above all else? And, for those who wish to confide in another, to be sure that their confidence is not misplaced before they speak.

THE SHARING

We told our stories –
That's all.
We sat and listened to
Each other
And heard the journeys
Of each soul.
We sat in silence
Entering each one's pain and
Sharing each one's joy.
We heard love's longing
And the lonely reachings-out
For love and affirmation.
We heard of dreams
Shattered
And visions fled.
Of hopes and laughter
Turned stale and dark.
We felt the pain of
Isolation and
The bitterness
Of death.

But in each brave and
Lonely story
God's gentle life
Broke through
And we heard music in
The darkness
And smelt flowers in
The void.

We felt the budding
Of creation
In the searchings of
Each soul

And discerned the beauty
Of God's hand in
Each muddy, twisted path.

And God's voice sang
In each story
His life sprang from
Each death.
Our sharing became
One story
Of a simple lonely search
For life and hope and
Oneness
In a world which sobs
For love.
And we knew that in
Our sharing
God's voice with
Mighty breath
Was saying
Love each other and
Take each other's hand.

For you are one
Though many
And in each of you
I live.
So listen to my story
And share my pain
And death.
Oh, listen to my story
And rise and live
With me.

Edwina Gateley

56

FOCUSING IN

Prayer and Pastoral Visiting

We cannot enjoy God without people. In this world God approaches us through people and can be seen in them. Jesus has assured us that in the next world heaven is a peopled place, though we have plenty of space – 'many rooms' – in which to be ourselves. Even hermits and members of enclosed orders draw aside partly in order to pray for the people of the world. So, interest in people is one way to grow towards God. This is what makes pastoral visiting so richly rewarding, because people have an infinite capacity to surprise us and in meeting them we shall encounter the mystery of God.

Focusing In is intended to support and encourage those who visit on behalf of the church, so that visiting can be more satisfying as a prayerful process. The pastoral carer need not feel alone but can become more aware of God's support and involvement in their care.

As we focus on people and their needs may we find God's presence beckoning to us as if through the image in the camera lens.

John D Walker

PRAYING WITH PEOPLE

THE VISIT – PRAYING WITH PEOPLE IN THEIR HOMES

On the threshold

One of the most time-honoured prayers on the doorstep, whether offered consciously or subconsciously, is the panicky feeling, 'O God – please let them be out!' However, we soon realise that an empty house would mean repeating the visit at another time or on another day. If the nervous feeling means that we are aware that we do not have instant answers to the whole range of human problems, then it is 'all right' – better than feeling over-confident and capable, which would put the person to be visited at a psychological disadvantage. The awkward moment may be avoided by telephoning to discover a mutually convenient time in advance – but sometimes the surprise element has pastoral advantages in that people have less opportunity to pre-arrange an acceptable public face and disguise their true needs and feelings. If the visitor prays at home for those to be visited and for a right approach, feelings of inadequacy or nervousness can be kept in check. The most important realisation is that God is in the situation before us – we do not presume to take him with us – we meet him there . . . He welcomes us over the threshold!

Luke 1:68   He has visited and redeemed his people.

Luke 10:5,6   Peace be to this house . . .

Mull over these two relevant texts and read them in their context to gain courage and purpose in visiting. How will God's people *know* that he has visited his people unless they hear your knock on the door? Should your regular prayer-on-the-doorstep be 'Peace be to this house'?

During the conversation

The giving and receiving of hospitality can be part of the prayer process, so if a cup of coffee or tea is offered and accepted it may not only oil the wheels of the conversation but be a visible expression of sharing. It is not always possible or healthy to accept every drink that is offered and the ability to decline firmly and politely gives integrity to the situation – but sometimes the person being visited has the need for the offer of simple hospitality to be accepted and would feel *personally* rejected if one of the early elements of the visit was a heavy, 'No, thank you'! Personal acceptance is part of the wonder of our relationship with

God – precisely the sense we wish to represent. This capacity to accept people as they are is one of the effects of our prayer life and vital for sensitive caring.

As the conversation develops and the various concerns, opportunities, disappointments, challenges and fears that the person or members of that household face gradually emerge, the visitor listens prayerfully by listening attentively, so that those who are pouring out their hearts know that they have been well and truly *heard*. Giving such undivided attention, asking for clarification when necessary, offering sympathy and drawing out a statement of the way things really are, without prying, is to give dignity and value to the person/persons being visited – a truly prayerful transaction.

While the conversation is taking place it can be helped along by short 'arrow' prayers to God, asking that the person/persons being visited may be set at ease, open up, say what they need to say and that one's own questions, comments and response may be perceptive and rightly fitted to the moment. Such arrow prayers could be 'God, please help me to say the right thing', or 'God, please let them trust me and open up', or simply 'God, help.'

Before leaving

On most occasions it is helpful, before leaving the home, to offer to pray with the person with whom one has been sharing. This open-ended offer could be made in words like, 'Shall we spend a moment in prayer together before I go?' In this way people do not feel pressurised into immediate prayer if they do not feel ready for it, or are not used to it, so that they can say 'no' without feeling tactless. It is also put in such a friendly tone that the visitor will not feel personally rejected if the answer is 'no'. However, most people, whether or not they are church-going, are often ready to say 'yes' and prayer sets a special seal on the quality of the relationship. In most settings, the prayer that is offered is simple and short and avoids pious phrases so that it feels natural and homely – personally tailored to the hopes and needs mentioned in the conversation. This is where careful listening pays dividends because the correct names of friends and family mentioned in conversation can be used, and problems can be accurately described in well-chosen words. Hesitations and grammar do not matter – sincerity does. We avoid suggesting neat answers to God and offer situations of need to his love for his solutions. Some people find 'free' extempore prayer difficult but it need not be. Short, simple, direct phrases which come naturally and avoid 'churchy' words are helpful because they do not sound stilted or artificial.   Sometimes a short memorised prayer can be more appropriate, such as:

> May the Lord bless you and keep you: the Lord make his face shine upon you, and be gracious unto you; the Lord lift up his countenance upon you, and give you peace.

> or:

> Grant us, in all our duties, your help;
> In all our perplexities, your guidance;
> In all our dangers, your protection;
> And in all our sorrows, your peace;
> Through Jesus Christ our Lord.
>
> *Saint Augustine*

Many church bookstalls and religious bookshops sell prayer cards which are attractively designed and can be left with the person we have visited as a parting gift to be used in a quiet moment. If the prayer is used together before parting, later use of the prayer card when the person is alone will recall and extend the benefit of the visit.

If the persons being visited seem at all uncomfortable at the suggestion of prayer, the idea can be usefully diverted by saying that we will remember them in our prayers each day while the problem lasts; this is both private and supportive. Some people are given extra support by being told the regular time at which we pray each day so that they may know that they are in our prayers just then. In some churches a prayer book listing the names of people in various kinds of need is kept up to date and we can ask permission to add the name of the person we are visiting to the list. In many local situations only the Christian name is used in the book to preserve some privacy. Alternative suggestions are to mention the Christian name at the next service of prayer for healing or to add the name to a list used by a local prayer fellowship or guild of health and healing. The likelihood is that to make one of the suggestions would be more helpful at a second or subsequent visit when good mutual confidence and rapport has been established.

After the visit

The visitor remembers the people and their needs in prayer and asks in prayer to be able to give them moral and prayerful support without brooding about their situations or being overshadowed by them. This will help us to gain something of the ideal pastoral balance, so that our prayer may be:

> WITH THE GREATEST OF CARE –
> LET GO
> LET GOD.
>
> *John D. Walker*

THE MINISTRY OF INTERCESSION

INTERCESSORY PRAYER – PRAYING FOR OTHER PEOPLE

Intercession is that aspect of prayer which is a reaching out in loving care for the needs of others. Charles Wesley caught the essence of intercession in his lines:

> Extend the arms of mighty prayer
> In grasping all mankind.
>
> *Hymns & Psalms 719*

Intercessory prayer is a way of life

The opening of that Wesley hymn is a direct quote from 1 Thess. 5:17, 'Pray without ceasing.' Many Christians down the centuries have puzzled over how to put Paul's words into effect. We understand that our whole being is to be so focused on God that every aspect of our life becomes part of a lived prayer. This helps us to become more integrated as persons, with more potential to reflect God's life and love to other people. Jesus says, 'Set your mind on God's kingdom and his justice before everything else' (Matt. 6:33). Prayer is a primary way by which we do this, an indispensable ingredient of our Christian vocation. Part of this ministry to which we are all called, but especially those with any kind of pastoral responsibility, is to pray on behalf of others, that in and through them God's kingdom may come.

Intercessory prayer embraces both the world and the individual

There are many people and situations for which we can only pray in a fairly general way – for refugees, for victims of war, earthquake or flood-disaster. But we will often pray too for a specific person whom we know, or have been told about. Whichever we are doing, certain things are basic:

Intercessory prayer is not telling God what to do!

We are not endeavouring to bend God to our will, but seeking to discover and work in harmony with his. God does not need persuading to act lovingly; he often uses us to help him to do so. We are praying to be 'a channel of his peace'. God is already present in a situation before we start to pray about it. Our prayer is that his presence may be recognised and responded to positively. At times we will hardly know what to pray for someone – but we can always pray for a person's healing and wholeness, and for peace in their life and relationships.

Intercessory prayer helps us to be more objective

If we are to express any loving care for a person, then we need to understand something of their situation; in some way to feel with them about their hopes and fears, about their areas of searching or dis-ease. This does not mean becoming prying busy-bodies, but just quietly reflecting on the person and their circumstances and holding them in our prayers before the God who loves equally and without reserve. In terms of our more general prayers of intercession, it means trying to keep ourselves informed about situations perhaps on the other side of the world, for example through what we watch or read.

Intercessory prayer will highlight our own attitudes

As we work away at trying to identify more deeply with those for whom we pray, we will inevitably be led into a greater awareness of ourselves. Strengths and weaknesses in our own personality and faith will be more sharply defined. Why are we praying for this other person? What are our expectations? Is there any element of our own possessiveness or dependency in what we are asking for them? Does the person with terminal cancer raise our own inner fears of dying, making us feel uncomfortable, so that we do not want to be involved? Are we able to pray that death itself may be received as part of God's healing gift?

SO HOW DO WE PRAY FOR OTHERS?

We begin by recognising God's longing for us to keep in touch with him. In our Methodist Communion Service we say, 'It is indeed right, it is our joy and salvation always and everywhere to give you thanks and praise.' There is real challenge in those words. It is easy when the sun is shining, but what about when we have just witnessed an accident, or are with someone receiving dreadful news? Always and everywhere . . . ? Yes, because God is present 'always and everywhere' and we are searching to see how God is present in that moment. 'Where are you, Lord?'

Then we should remember that wherever we are and whatever is happening, all is contained within the love of God. In that same Communion prayer we go on to say, 'Bring us with the whole creation to your heavenly kingdom.' Nothing is outside God's creative love and there is no situation, however terrible, through which God cannot work. 'In everything the Spirit co-operates for good with those who love God' (Romans 8:28).

Recognise that you are sharing in a real ministry

As we have already seen, making intercession on behalf of others is part of our vocation as Christians. Exactly how we express that vocation varies enormously, according to our personality and also to the point where we are in life. People who may consider themselves limited by advancing age or infirmity or handicap may find a renewed sense of self-worth in becoming involved in a ministry of intercessory prayer. Intercession undertaken in partnership with another person, or with a small group or network of pray-ers, can be an extra source of strength. How to work alongside others in this way is well worth exploring, for it increases both our sense of obligation to pray regularly and our awareness of mutual support. If we are not able actually to meet with others, we might agree on a common time of intercession, creating a network of prayer.

Be consistent

Prayer is like the waves on the shore. It is a quiet rhythm of drawing down into the depths of God, that we may be cast up on the shores of life with renewed strength. A regular pattern of intercessory prayer is part of that rhythm. We might try making a list of different topics for different days of the week – one day for those in serious illness, another day for those with relationship difficulties and so on. It is helpful to have a pattern like this written out as a reminder.

Don't be over-ambitious

We cannot pray in depth for every aspect of human need. Be content with a short list of people for whom to pray. Review the list regularly, and create it afresh perhaps once a month. Here again, to do this in association with other people who are praying for the same particular situations can deepen our sense of the fellowship of the prayers of the people of God.

Always be courteous

Our prayers for others must never violate their privacy or demean them as persons. If we share prayer concerns with someone else, then we must be very careful not to betray things which may have been told to us in confidence. We should pause too before we foist our prayers on other people unasked. It might be more helpful to enquire first, 'Would you like me/us to pray for you?'

Remember that intercession is part of your larger prayer life

Prayer for others goes alongside and is sustained by our worship, public and private, by our adoration and meditation, by our own drawing apart to be with him who is the life of the world.

David Nash

Eternal God,
whose will is to fulfil all things in
    Christ;
receive the prayers we offer for others
    in their need,
and in the knowledge of your saving
    presence
may they find strength and peace.

God of love,
let your love be known this day
by each for whom in love I pray.

PRAYING IN COMMUNITY

The disciples recognised that prayer played an important part in the life of Jesus. We read that on one occasion, after Jesus had spent time in prayer, his disciples said to him:

Lord, teach us to pray, as John taught his disciples.

Jesus replied with a model prayer, the Lord's Prayer, and teaching on perseverance in prayer (Luke 11:1-13). The disciples wanted to know how to pray because they saw Jesus at prayer.

Today many Christians admit that they need help with their prayer life. They see those who seem to find prayer easy and natural and wonder why this is not true of their experience. They may rely on the Christian community to do their praying for them and may come to appreciate that the 'voice of prayer is never silent' *(Hymns & Psalms 648)*. However, unless they can be freed from a sense of guilt which comes from feelings of inadequacy or neglect in the life of prayer, prayer may never come alive for them.

While some may find it easier to pray as individuals, others discover that prayer only has significance for them in the context of Christian worship. In many ways the prayers offered in worship are like the tip of the iceberg, the public offering of prayers representing the dedication and faithfulness of God's people with the hint that there is much more prayer activity below the surface.

A number of insights are given through sharing together in prayer:

1. To pray in community means that all have a chance to participate. What happens in church when the words 'Let us pray' are spoken? Is that the time to switch off and have a rest in the middle of a service? Or is it the time when those present concentrate their thoughts on God's love and the particular issues which concern them, so that prayer is a source of vibrant power in that community? The beauty of prayer is that all can contribute, whether as beginners or mature students in the school of prayer.

2. To pray in community means that periods of silence are used positively. Prayer can easily become one way traffic when God's voice is effectively drowned out by the flood of requests made to him. There has to be time for lives to be opened up to God so that a right relationship with him can be cultivated. Christians ask for what they

67

want in prayer against the background of a relationship they already enjoy with God.

3.   To pray in community can help remove obstacles to prayer. It is so easy for Christians to be wrapped up in themselves in the life of prayer. There is always this danger of privatising prayer and the praying community can provide an effective deterrent to this tendency. There is also the danger of using prayer as a form of escapism, a running away from the real world.   The hymnwriter warns us about this and concludes:

> May our prayers, Lord, make us
> Ten times more aware
> That the world we banish
> Is our Christian care.

(Fred Pratt Green)

Prayer can, of course, be deadened by disobedience, when Christians keep on asking for what they want but constantly ignore what God wants from them. The Christian community can challenge each individual to be obedient to God through prayers offered in faith.

4.   To pray in community is an opportunity to share in God's purpose. Mark tells a story about four people who carried a paralysed man to Jesus for healing. When they were unable to get close because of the crowd, the friends opened up the roof and lowered the man into the presence of Jesus. As a result of their faith the paralysed man received forgiveness and healing.
The praying community offers its prayers trusting in the one to whom it prays and knowing that he hears and answers prayers. One of the privileges of the Christian community is to bring people into the presence of Christ through its intercessions.

There are a number of ways of doing this and circumstances will determine the appropriate methods.

a) Sunday Worship. This is the main time when people gather together to pray and this prayer time in public worship ought to be used creatively and imaginatively. If prayer is seen as a solo effort on these occasions, with no space for people to make an appropriate contribution to the intercessions, then an opportunity has been missed. Pauses for reflection between prayers or periods of silence helpfully introduced can help to involve people in the prayer life of the church community. The psalms or the petitions and intercessions in the service book can be useful aids.

b) Extended Communion. Pastoral visitors may take the bread and the wine from a service in church to the sick or the housebound, as another way of involving more members of the Christian community in the fellowship of prayer.

c) Prayer Services. There are churches which hold weekly or monthly midweek services with the focus on intercessions. Some are linked with a coffee morning while others take place in the evening. Often these services are Communion services.

d) Prayer Partners. People are invited to add their names to a list and so sign on as partners in prayer, committing themselves to a form of disciplined praying. Sometimes this approach is linked with a prayer diary or evangelistic outreach in the life of the church.

e) A Prayer Book. People are invited to write their prayer requests in a book at the entrance to the church The book is offered up with the collection and prayers are included in the intercessions during the worship.

f) A Prayer Box. This can be used in the same way as a Prayer Book or in the intercessions at a service during the week. Some churches have regular meetings for prayer or a healing service when intercessions can be included.

g) A Prayer Board. This can be an effective means of prayer when a church is open and accessible to people who want to share their concerns in this way.

h) Prayer Candles. A number of churches are now using candles to encourage worshippers to come forward to light a candle and to offer prayer, spoken or unspoken.

David Willie

* * * *

SILENCE IN PASTORAL VISITING

The silence we are thinking about is not the absence of noise, but space in which we can become aware of God. Many people know very little about entering into silence; they may feel apprehensive and need to be reassured that it is not uncomfortable. When we are visiting we often come across people living alone who look to Christian fellowship for help and conversation: they can be helped to discover that silence can change loneliness into solitude. Silence can be renewing. People who find silence easy need to be aware of the needs of others who find it more difficult.

The silence that is ours

Silence is a special gift from God that we can share with one another. Jesus shared his gift with the disciples who, when watching him at prayer, requested that he teach them to pray (Luke 11:1-4). He responded by giving them words and phrases that lend themselves to meditation. Reflecting on the relevant words of the Lord's Prayer is a way of being silent in our prayer time. We can also introduce silence into prayer with a verse from scripture, or a line of a hymn, and say it over to ourselves a few times until we feel a sense of quiet. We might use:

Peace is what I leave with you, it is my peace
that I give to you. *(John 14:27)*

or:

Jesus Christ is Lord. *(Phil. 2:11)*

Another way is to plan a few moments of silence in our prayer time. Wesley's hymn *Hymns & Psalms* 540 is useful, especially the words:

> Silent am I now and still,
> Dare not in thy presence move;
> To my waiting soul reveal
> The secret of thy love.

Perhaps when reading a Bible passage a word or phrase will light up. Should this happen, we do not have to read the whole passage, but can stay with that word or phrase and let it penetrate into our inner consciousness. We can try to clear our mind of all the clutter that is there and remain still and silent in the presence of God. Here something to hold or a picture to look at may help.

Centreing ourselves in times of silence becomes an experience we take into our daily lives.

Taking silence into the homes we visit

Our inner focus of silence goes with us when we visit. We can't be consciously praying all the time; we carry with us the presence of God. Sometimes when we visit we are, perhaps, rather more conscious of our own feelings and anxieties than we are of this inner stillness. We can also be concerned about saying the right things, how to approach someone bereaved or facing family problems.

Jesus recognised that we might be filled with a sense of foreboding and promised that his Holy Spirit would be with us (John 14:16). We may need a moment or two to remind ourselves of his promise and connect with our own inner silence. This is not always easy to do; we each find our own way. We can snatch a few moments for quiet reflection before knocking on the door, or take time to quieten ourselves. One way of doing this is to listen to the natural rhythm of our breathing. Another way is to remind ourselves of some words of Jesus, such as:

> You did not choose me, I chose you and appointed you to go
> out. *(John 15:16)*

Silence in one's own interior life is somehow helping people to recognise that the peace of God is within them.

Silence in prayer

When we are visiting and prayer seems appropriate, silence can be introduced within the prayer. We need to be aware of the other person's feelings and sense whether they are likely to be comfortable with silence. A simple way of introducing silence near the beginning of the prayer is to say:

Let us be quiet for a moment and remember God is with us . . .

then be quiet for a few moments. Within the prayer there may be an opportunity of offering the feelings that emerged in the conversation. We are giving people the opportunity to bring these feelings to God in the silence. When we are visiting we will come across people who love the opportunity to chatter happily about their lives and families. Someone living alone might tell you how thrilled they were to receive an unexpected letter, or how special it is for them that a neighbour's cat will often come in for a saucer of milk. They have something to celebrate and we can enable them to do that in the silence.

Sharing silence unites where words can divide.

Silence with another person

It is not only in prayer that silence is important, it also has a place in our conversations in the silence of listening. To be with someone in silence can be a way of reaching out to them in love. Jesus did this. When faced with Martha's outburst *(Luke 10:38-42)*, he did not intervene, giving her the opportunity to release all the frustration she felt before he spoke to her. Occasionally, when we are visiting, someone may wish to unburden their feelings. For example, if they express a sense of guilt, it is not going to help if we interrupt and say there is nothing to feel guilty about. At that moment they are feeling guilty, whatever we might think about it. Our silence gives them the opportunity to release some of their feelings. It can also help if we hold that silence. Sometimes we visit people who are very ill or in particular need and words are inappropriate to the situation; then it is right just to sit quietly with them. Touch is often a help during such silences. Jesus requested those closest to him to be with him in silence when he knelt to pray in the garden. *(Matt 26:38)*

Silence can be a kind of echo chamber offering space and reflection on what has been said.

Let the last word come from someone who was visited. The illustration is taken from *View from a Hearse* by Job Baylys. After the death of one of his children, he was sitting, torn by grief, when someone called and talked. Remarking on how he felt, the bereaved man said, 'I was unmoved and wished he would go away.' Another visitor came and sat with him in silence and prayed simply. The father commented, 'I was moved, I was comforted, I hated to see him go.'

Silent prayers

Look at the words of Isaiah (49:16). Instead of Jerusalem substitute your name and consider what it means not to be forgotten, to be known by name, and for that name to be written in the palm of God's hand.

Another passage that lends itself to silence is Paul's words in Eph (3:14-19). Read the passage through once or twice and see which words you are drawn to and meditate on those for a few moments.

Margaret Hale

PRAYING WITH SYMBOLS

The use of symbols can deepen and enlarge our understanding of pastoral ministry and can lead us into new and unexpected ways of entering into our own and other people's experience.

God has given us imagination and intuition as well as an ability to reason and think logically. As we seek to give and receive care we need to allow all our gifts of sensitivity and perception to inform and *trans*form our ministry of practical, reasoned care and friendship for one another. Only then shall we be truly present to each other.

Words in themselves are never fully adequate for expressing how we feel about others or about God. Sometimes, through symbols that are appropriate for us, we can catch glimpses, sense a communication, an empathy, that words and thoughts on their own deny us.

You will discover symbols which mean a great deal to you. In the following passages I share some symbols which have had a profound influence on my own pastoral understanding. They can only be pointers and suggestions because what speaks to me will not necessarily move you in the same way. And a symbol that is important for us at one stage of our experience may prove dull and lifeless at another. So much of the power of symbolism lies in its ability to open up for us new possibilities and fresh understanding. Symbols never allow us to remain static for very long!

CANDLES

As I write there is a lighted candle in front of me, a candle which was brought as a gift from the Peace Chapel of the Central Methodist Mission in Johannesburg. Some years ago I heard the minister from that church, Peter Storey, speak most movingly of the way in which the congregation there lit their Amnesty Candle every week as they prayed for relatives and friends in prison and detention, and as a result I resolved that before lunch-time every Sunday we, too, would light a candle to symbolise the fact that our thoughts and prayers were with that congregation and with their whole nation in its struggle for justice and peace. This we did as a family wherever we were, and consequently we went through a number of candles by the time apartheid was finally declared illegal! – but as we lit them our understanding was illuminated in ways we could never have envisaged.

Those candles became a means and focus of intercession; they became symbols of love and support and solidarity, an incentive to practical support and an inspiration for us to try to enter into the same struggle against injustice in our own context. Lighting our candles showed us that symbols, like candlelight, have many facets. There is vulnerability in a candle flame – it can easily be extinguished; but with care and attention the flame can be relit and when it is alight, fragile though it is, it illuminates an area far beyond itself. There is warmth, too, and colour in the glow of a candle but there is also a changing pattern which reminds us that life is never static and that, as the flame points upwards, we need to remember to offer all our endeavours and hopes up to God. Or, in different vein, a candle can mean what it does to Samuel Rayan, an Indian poet:

> A candle-light is a protest at midnight,
> It is non-conformist.
> It says to the darkness,
> 'I beg to differ.'

Within many churches candles are lit as signs of prayer for individuals or particular concerns. I lit a candle in All Saints Church, Margaret Street, when 91 year old Janet, who had been a friend and teacher since teenage years, died. She had loved worshipping in that church and my candle seemed to be the right symbol, not simply of thanksgiving and hope, but also of the ongoing life of the Communion of Saints and of the promise, 'The light shines in the darkness and the darkness has never put it out.'

Whole communities use candles as their symbols, either deliberately or spontaneously. A report in *The Times* in 1976 gives this account:

Hiroshima, August 6th. Hundreds of candles representing the souls of Hiroshima's atomic bomb victims shine in the dusk over a Japanese river tonight in a moving climax to ceremonies commemorating the dropping of the bomb 31 years ago.

The candles, in small wood and paper lanterns with peace messages on them, were set adrift in the Ota river from the memorial park in the city centre . . .

So, as the light has been shining from the candle in front of me it has already taken me across the world and brought me home again. It has spoken of individuals both living and dead, known and unknown. It has reminded me of the depths to which human beings can sink, yet it has pointed me upwards towards the light and purity of God. It has built bridges, it has made friends at a deep level, it has nudged me into practical action and it has proved an inspiration for lighting other candles of one kind or another. If that is what one candle can achieve as a symbol, what a tremendously imaginative and significant difference it could make to our lives as a whole if we allowed all the things of God's world to be signs and symbols, bringing us closer to an understanding of his love and his intention and will for us and for others.

SIGNS OF CARE

To think about . . . and pray about.

Does my church care for families realistically?

Do we 'walk together' as a community or do some feel excluded from the church family?

How do we befriend those who seem to see no light at the end of the 'tunnel' they are in at present?

Do I have problems myself which seem insoluble?
Do I need to share them with a trusted friend?

We all need to be alone at times yet no-one wants to be lonely. Pray for those whom you believe to be lonely. Can you or your church do anything to help?

Try to enter into the actual needs of those who are elderly or disabled, and not to assume that they are the ones you would expect.

Think about all the good things you have received from those who are older than you are, or from those who live with chronic illness or disability.

Think about your own work situation. Pray for those with whom you work, especially those you find difficult and unfriendly. Pray for anyone you know who is out of work or is unhappy in the job they do.

ROSES

I have a bed of 'Blessings' in my garden and in summer these lovely roses are, for me, a constant symbol of the church's pastoral ministry. Through the warmth of their colour, their fragility, their fragrance, their open petals, sharp thorns, green leaves, and as a sign of love, they speak of life's pain and vulnerability. And in their need for light from the sun, refreshing rain and good soil for their roots

they symbolise each person's need for careful tending and for the right personal and social conditions if they are to achieve their full potential.

The actual names of roses are often significant in terms of pastoral ministry – Johnnie Walker, Hannah Gordon, Anne Harkness, Grandpa Dickson – for we are all individuals, unique in both needs and gifts and special because of our particular characteristics.

Evocative, too, are the roses whose names have a particular connotation:

Pensioner's Voice – which poses the question – How do we respond to those who are older in our society? Do we recognise not only their needs but also their ongoing ability to contribute within church and society?

Loving Memory – bereavement is not the only area of loss we have to negotiate. All change leaves us with memories and difficult adjustments as well as offering us fresh possibilities. We need each other's prayers in all situations.

Prosperity – what is our social commitment on behalf of those who are homeless or poor or disadvantaged? What kind of 'prosperity' and wholeness do we want for people, ourselves included?

The Observer – do we try to observe, to see people as they really are, or do we project our own prejudices and insecurities on to them? Are we prepared to listen to people with our eyes and with our hearts as well as with our ears?

Studdert Kennedy began one of his poems with the words:

There is a world of wonder in this rose.

We simply need the vision to see it in all its glory and truth.

PEBBLES

Practical suggestions:

- Collect some different shaped pebbles from your garden or pebbles from the beach.

- Sit quietly in your room and hold a pebble in your hand, using it as a focus for your praying.

- Give your feelings of heaviness and regret to the pebbles.

- Remember that your pebble is part of creation and try to imagine all that may have happened to it over the centuries.

- Feel the way it has been shaped by ice and flood, by being broken and by being re-fashioned.

- Look at it in detail. Feel its surface. Notice what is special about it – what special markings it has. Be aware of its rough edges.

- Imagine what will happen to it next. Will it be put to good use or will it be used in a destructive way?

- Gradually allow it to speak to you of your own experience. Think back over your own life, your own journey to this point. What is special about you? What are your 'rough edges'? Your interesting and beautiful qualities? And what future possibilities are there for you?

- Place your pebble in a bowl of water and as you watch its colours become more defined ask God to refresh and cleanse you and surround you with his love, so that you may become more clearly his.

OR:

- Take one of the pebbles that in some way reminds you of someone who has had a deep influence on you for good.

- Meditate on that person's qualities. What was it that made them special?

- You might choose a small rounded pebble which reminds you of a person who was apparently of little significance in other people's eyes, or was little in stature, yet whose radiance of life or gentleness of spirit touched all with whom they came in contact.

- You might choose a large well-rounded pebble which spoke to you of someone's consistency – their loyalty – or their 'wholeness'.

- The pebbles are there for your choosing. What does your choice of pebble say to you in your role as a pastoral carer?

OR:

You may wish simply to hold a small pebble in your hand as you meditate on Julian of Norwich's beautiful words:

> He is our clothing, for love; He enwraps us and envelops us, embraces us and encloses us; He hovers over us, for tender love, that He may never leave us . . .
> In this He shewed me a little thing, the quantity of a hazel nut, lying in the palm of my hand, and to my understanding it was as round as any ball. I looked thereupon and thought: 'What may this be?' And I was answered in a general way thus: 'It is all that is made.' I marvelled how it could last, for methought it might fall suddenly to naught for littleness. And I was answered in my understanding: 'It lasts and ever shall last because God loves it, and so hath all-thing its being through the love of God.'
> In this little thing I saw three parts. The first is God made it; the second is that He loves it; the third that He keeps it. **But what is that to me? Insooth, the Maker, the Lover, the Keeper.**

Jesus, take me as I am,
I can come no other way.
Take me deeper into you,
Make my flesh life melt away.
Make me like a precious stone,
Crystal clear and finely-honed.
Life of Jesus, shining through,
Giving glory back to you.

*Dave Bryant**

* * * *

As Christians we are at home with symbols. In our corporate
worship we meet together and sing:

Here are symbols to remind us
Of our lifelong need of grace;
Here are table, font and pulpit,
Here the cross has central place.

Fred Pratt Green

All around us, at all times, there are symbols reminding us not only
of our need of grace but also of God's loving response to that need.
There is 'grace abounding' if we will but look for it and open our hearts
to receive it. A ring, a handshake, a shoe symbolising a journey, a kiss,
the giving of the peace – all these and many more can be significant
symbols of God's presence in our world. We need to explore their
meaning and value for us, knowing that the more we allow God's grace
and love to penetrate us in this way the more gracious and loving our
pastoral ministry in relationship with others will become.

Ann Bird

TRADITIONAL PASTORAL PRAYERS

Praying with people:

Here are some old prayers of the Church which sum up in a few words some of the key things which will often come out of a visit. Don't be afraid of reading prayers: it is helpful to get the words right, and you could put too much pressure on yourself by trying to learn them off by heart – however well you remember words in the familiar setting of your own home, it is not worth the pressure of forgetting when you are helping someone else through your prayers. One way to use them would be to have them copied out and then you could leave a copy behind when you left.

It might also be helpful to read a Psalm: some possible ones could be: 19, 24, 34, 42, 46, 90, 95, 100, 103

General prayers:

> Almighty God,
> you have taught us through your Son
> that love is the fulfilling of the law.
> Grant that we may love you with our whole heart
> and our neighbours as ourselves;
> through Jesus Christ our Lord.   Amen.

> Almighty God,
> you have made us for yourself
> and our hearts are restless
> till they find their final rest in you;
> teach us to offer ourselves to your service
> that here we may have your peace
> and in the world to come may see you face to face;
> through Jesus Christ our Lord.   Amen.

Prayers for guidance:

O God,
you know us to be set
in the midst of so many and great dangers,
that by reason of the frailty of our nature
we cannot always stand upright:
grant us such strength and protection
as may support us in all dangers
and carry us through all temptations;
through Jesus Christ our Lord. Amen.

Eternal God
whose Son Jesus Christ
is the way, the truth and the life;
grant us to walk in his way,
to rejoice in his truth,
and to share his risen life;
who is alive and reigns with you and the Holy Spirit,
one God, now and for ever. Amen.

Prayers to face the future:

Almighty and everlasting God,
increase in us your gift of faith;
that forsaking what lies behind
and reaching out to that which is before,
we may run the way of your commandments
and win the crown of everlasting joy;
through Jesus Christ our Lord. Amen.

Merciful God,
you have prepared for those who love you
such good things as pass our understanding;
pour into our hearts such love towards you
that we, loving you above all things,
may obtain your promises,
which exceed all that we can desire,
through Jesus Christ our Lord. Amen.

Celtic prayers

May the eye of the great God
– the God of glory,
– the Virgin's Son
– the gentle Spirit
Aid you and shepherd you
    in every time;
Pour upon you every hour
Lovingly and generously.

In our hearts and this house
The blessing of God
In our life and believing
The love of God
In our meeting with friend and stranger
The peace of God
In our end, as at our beginning
The arms of God to welcome us and bring us home.

The guarding of the God of life be here;
The guarding of the Caring Christ be here;
The guarding of the Spirit be on this place
Every day and at every night
To aid us and enfold us.

Don Pickard

PASTORAL PRAYERS OF TODAY

Prayers that could be used or adapted in pastoral visiting.

Thoughts before visiting:

Why me, Lord?

> Be still
> and remember how much I love you.
> You go in my name,
> in my strength.
> There, you will meet with me.
> I am already with those people,
> they are my loved ones.

What have I got to offer?

> All I have is yours.
> Go humbly,
> offer friendship.
> Allow my peace within you
> to touch troubled hearts.
> Listen deeply.
> Speak gently.
> Love greatly.

> O God of faithfulness and love
> I go in your strength, to be a servant
> in the name of Jesus Christ. Amen.

A prayer before visiting:

Compassionate God, you know and understand the people I shall meet today.

Help me to offer:

space	–	in which they may feel valued and loved;
patience	–	to listen to sacred stories;
compassion	–	to recognise deep needs;
sensitivity	–	to the prompting of your Spirit;
warmth	–	to convey your faithfulness and love.

Gracious God, may people catch a glimpse of the face of Jesus Christ in me and understand that he is with them.

Bless me, that I may be a blessing to others. Amen.

A prayer for those coping with problems, those feeling wounded by life:

> The Spirit of God is with us.
>   (pause for a few moments)
>
> Loving God
>   who loves and knows us as no other;
>   who takes our brokenness and heals;
>   who takes our diversity and unites.
> Give us, in our brokenness
>   a desire, to know Jesus the healer;
>   courage, to embrace the pain in his strength;
>   the will, to live and love again;
> that we may celebrate your goodness and mercy,
> your tenderness and strength,
> to the glory of Jesus our Saviour. Amen.

A prayer for those suffering bereavement, coping with grief:

> Gracious God, you speak tenderly to your children and understand when we pass through the dark places of life. Lighten the darkness of this present moment by helping us to know that you have not left us alone.
>
> Compassionate God, you are with us in the shedding of our tears, in the remembering of happy as well as painful times, and in the task of coming to terms with those changes in life over which we have no control.
>
> Surround us with companions for this stage of our pilgrimage. Enable us to help others in their distress. Give us each day the strength and patience we need. Keep us and those we know, on earth and in heaven, within your loving care.
>
> Take us by the hand and help us as we stumble.
> Draw us gently to you, as a mother sustaining her young.
> Cover us with your peace, enfold us in your heart of love.

Be with us, behind us and before us, today and always. Amen.

A simple blessing:

As the coming of dawn –
    may your faith in God be born anew each day.
As the touch of the wind on your face –
    may you know the caress of God's love.
As the hand of a child slips into the hand of the one who loves –
    may you travel with God.

A prayer for those who are 'OK', those who are busy but who rejoice in life, sharing in the joys and sorrows of the world

(Pick up from your conversation with them or ask for the needs of others to be included in prayer. This might be family or neighbourhood needs, prayers for the Church, particular people to be named.)

Loving God, we are thankful for this moment in time when, within the fellowship of your love, we can pause to voice our worship and praise, acknowledging that we are your children and that you are with us.

We praise you for your loveliness revealed to us in Jesus Christ and for your goodness and mercy to us throughout life. We are aware of the many blessings which surround us:

the love of family and friends;
the fellowship of the Church;'
the beauty of your world;
the kindness of strangers;
the opportunity to help others.

We are aware of those who lack such blessings:

the lonely and bereaved;
the homeless and friendless;
those living in tragic circumstances;
those unable to trust the people around them;
those lacking the basics of life which give dignity.

We pray for all who face major decisions or life events;

> men and women who sustain and nurture family life;
> those who give leadership in Church and nation;
> those who make make-or-break decisions regarding peace on earth.

We pray that all people may know the blessings of your love. Help us sensitively to share the resources of the world with our neighbours and be channels of encouragement and peace.

* * * *

> God of the pilgrim way,
> travel with us on our journey;
> be with us at every turn of the road,
> draw us ever closer to you.
> Make glad our hearts with the radiance of your love;
> nurture our understanding of your faithfulness,
> that our security may be only in your goodness and mercy,
> through Jesus Christ our Lord. Amen.

Christine Walters

CARING MATTERS

SEEING CLEARLY

A cartoon, which I frequently use in workshops, shows two people sitting on a bench back to back and keeping a safe distance from each other. They are not touching. They are not looking at one another. They are clearly not communicating with each other on any real level at all. This fact is underlined by the captions ballooning from their mouths. One reads, 'I'm not talking to you', the other reads, 'That's OK. I'm not listening.' Some time ago when I was on a bereavement counselling course we were asked to sit back to back in a manner reminiscent of the cartoon, and we were then asked to share something of importance to us with the other person for ten minutes each. It was one of the hardest exercises we were called upon to do but it taught us many things.

First and foremost it gave us a tiny inkling of what it must be like to be blind and to have to concentrate on what is said with particular intensity because a blind person cannot listen with their eyes as can a sighted person. It also made us realise how much we depend upon seeing another person's expression and body language when we are trying to listen sensitively to what they are saying to us. For those of us who are sighted, seeing and being seen is all a part of the listening process. We communicate with our eyes and we recognise symptoms of distress or happiness or uncertainty by noticing people's expressions and behaviour and we respond accordingly.

What we must be careful to guard against, though, is making glib and therefore often false assumptions when we think we are 'seeing' someone. After all we are ourselves well practised at putting on a mask, afraid to let people come too close to the person we really are, and at times it is right and proper that we should protect our privacy and identity in this way. We choose the moments when we feel safe enough to reveal who we really are to other people and most of us will choose moments when we have been made to feel that we shall remain acceptable and cherished whatever confidences or truths we may disclose.

Knowing this, as those who want to encourage others to feel safe in our company, we need to learn to look beyond outward appearance – not in a prying or intrusive way – but because we genuinely want to know and appreciate the person behind the mask, to discover what it is that makes them special in the eyes of God. It is so easy to be put off by someone who appears to be different from us – someone who is not our 'type', who dresses differently, who looks as if they are brimming with confidence and security. Yet it is the variety in God's world that makes it so rich in beauty and possibility and in all our diversity we human beings all have one thing in common – the need to love and to be loved. But because we are such vulnerable creatures it is only when we are met by gentleness and acceptance that we dare to begin to let the masks slips a little and to allow other people to see us as we really are, confused maybe, probably not always very nice, often insecure but nevertheless full of potential for sharing, for friendship and for growth in terms of relationship.

I have a piece of wood which is carved in such a way that at first glance all one can see are a number of strips of light wood set against a dark wooden background. For those who can see the whole piece in perspective and who look beyond the light wood on the surface the word JESUS becomes clearly apparent. I thought I knew how to look at it so that I could automatically see the hidden word, but on one occasion I was taken aback when I saw a similar carving and only figured out the word EMMANUEL in the background with great difficulty and much screwing up of eyes and tilting of head! Was it because I thought I knew what I was going to see? Was it that I was not as skilled at looking as I had believed myself to be? Was it that my mind wasn't really on what I was doing? Whatever the reason, my failure prompted me to recognise again that we can never be complacent enough to think that we have in some way mastered the art of seeing another person. Every person is different. Every meeting of any real depth with another person involves our looking afresh at the person and the situation and requires, too, a recognition that life and relationships are far too complex for us ever to imagine that we have ever, as it were, 'got the whole picture'.

Listening with our eyes takes practice as much as does looking at the popular three-dimensional pictures that are everywhere on cards, in books, on posters, and even now on T-shirts! To see people and situations in depth, in context and in focus requires patience, a lack of pre-conceived notions and a willingness to adjust our perceptions – as well as a willingness to realise that we never really see *ourselves* properly, let alone other people!

There are other aspects of seeing which are vital to us if we are to be imaginative people who 'see into the life of things'. In Truro Cathedral one summer there was a fascinating display of pictures by an artist called Cecil Riley. One painting in particular caught and held my attention. It was a beautifully painted watercolour entitled 'Noah smells the flowers'. The floods had receded, the ark was perched precariously on the Ararat mountains in the distance, and Noah sat on the grass gazing with loving attention at the delicate beauty of the riot of flowers around him.

It is a picture I shall not forget. It took me beyond its immediate attraction to remind me of the beauty that surrounds us all in so many ways and of the blessing and healing which flows from drawing that beauty into oneself as far as is possible. It evoked a longing to look again at everything in life and to see with new eyes, to acknowledge the possibilities hidden within each moment and each encounter and to look at life, and people in particular, with the kind of loving attention that Noah offered even to the most apparently insignificant flower he held in his hand.

Yet I know I can only look in this way with God's help. If I am afraid of being hurt or becoming too involved with others I shall not only shut myself up from them I shall shut myself away from God, for we cannot be truly open to him and closed to others. Whether we like it or not vision and vulnerability are intertwined and if, for one reason or another, we refuse really to see someone else, we distance ourselves from seeing God's presence in our lives as well.

The little prince in the book of that name by St. Exupéry says, 'In your world, men cultivate five thousand roses in one garden and still they do not find what they seek. And yet what they are seeking may be found in a single rose or a drop of water . . . but the eyes are blind – one must seek with the heart.' So too our listening to one another and to God is a seeking – and a seeing – with the heart. It is a seeing beneath the surface so that people begin to be glimpsed as they really are. It is a listening which invites us to face each other and see in each other a unique miracle made in the image of God and created for eternal life. It involves seeing God's presence everywhere in the world, not least in each individual we meet ,and encourages us to welcome and value people as they are so that all who wish to respond to our offer of friendship and loving care feel safe to do so.

Ann Bird

i) Watch either:
a soap opera, eg. *Neighbours, EastEnders, Coronation Street*, etc.

or:

a studio discussion programme, eg. *Question Time, Heart of the Matter,* etc.

What emotions do you assume are being expressed by the individuals as you observe body position/posture, facial expressions, use of hands, general movement?

Were these situations comfortable/uncomfortable, friendly/unfriendly? Did you find your feelings affected as you watched? How did you feel?

ii) Repeat this exercise by watching a stranger from a distance, eg. at work, in a shop, etc.

SEEING WITH LOVE

Dear God,
teach us to see people
with loving attention
– never to dismiss a neighbour
as a problem, a case,
a bungler, an inadequate,
a go-getter, a high-flier . . .
For a label says so much less
than the truth about someone.
So teach us to look past
the label;
give us a compassionate curiosity
about the rest of the story.

    If I can see myself
    through the eyes of someone
    who loves me,
    I stop running away from myself.
    If I can learn
    that I am valued and respected,
    I can forgive myself, and grow.
So give us the wisdom
to see when we might be judging others
or using their failings
to bolster our own self-esteem.
Teach us to listen with stillness
to the hurts that have shaped them.
And if some word of challenge is needed,
then prevent us from disabling people
with our criticism;
rather, help us to question the deeds
whilst accepting the doers,
and to see with the eyes of Christ
their potential for growth and greatness.

Kate Compston

94

iii) To what extent does the seeing – or not seeing – of the face hidden above parallel believing – or not believing – in God?

iv) Do you sometimes feel as though other people's perception of you is very different from your own perception of yourself?

If possible, spend time walking silently in the garden, in a park, in the countryside. Open your senses to God. Listen to the sounds around you. Touch a flower, a leaf, a pebble. Be aware of your feelings. Look at things closely. Reflect on the experience.

If you wish to enter the world of those
who are broken or closed in upon themselves,
it is important to learn their language.

Learning a language
is not just learning French or Spanish or German.
It is learning to understand what people are really
saying,
the non-verbal as well as the verbal language.

The verbal, exterior language is the beginning
and is absolutely necessary,
but you must go deeper
and discover what it means to listen:
to listen deeply to another,
to the cry flowing from the heart,
in order to understand people,
both in their pain and in their gift;
to understand what they are truly asking
so that you can hold their wound, their pain
and all that flows from it:
    violence, anger or depression,
    self-centredness and limitless demands;
    the suffocating urge to possess,
    the refusal to let go;
to accept these with compassion,
without judging, without condemning.

You must go deeper and discover
what it really means to see another!
    – to see the light shining in the darkness,
    – to recognize the seeds of hidden gifts
and to water these seeds and rejoice as they grow.

Jean Vanier

* * * *

*Perceptive Jesus, open my eyes that I may notice the needs of others and see the
signs of your presence in all around me. Amen.*

ACTING RESPONSIBLY

1995 was a year of memories, a year when the ending of the second world war was much in our minds and when VE and VJ Day elicited countless reflections about the past and renewed determination about the future. In the midst of all the national 'remembering' our local church took time during one morning service to recall the life and ministry of one of its former members, Leslie Burgin, who died just as the war finally came to a close.

There were particular reasons for this time of recollection. Leslie Burgin was a very gifted man, a lawyer, holding high positions on many councils and committees and an outstanding athlete as well as being a local preacher; but it was as a Member of Parliament and particularly as Minister of Transport in Neville Chamberlain's coalition government, as well as the minister delegated to set up the Ministry of Supply in 1939, that he was known in the wider world. After his death, his family commissioned a beautiful stained glass window in his memory which was installed at the west end of the church and designed by Frank Salisbury, who was himself a member of the church and renowned at the time for his windows and paintings in many of England's great cathedrals. So on August 20th 1995, fifty years on, we were asked as a congregation to turn round to face this window and look at it as part of our prayer time and as an acknowledgement that so much that Leslie Burgin stood for in public life was still of total relevance in today's world.

The window has four lights with figures representing Nature, Justice, Law and Service. Nature is represented by a young shepherd; Justice by a warrior with sword unsheathed ready to defend the right; Law by a figure of mature understanding holding the book of law; and Service by a woman shouldering great responsibilities.

As I stood there I found myself relating the separate images to all the pastoral involvement which goes beyond our pastoral interaction with individuals and which leads us into social and political action on behalf of others and of community life in all its aspects. The image of the shepherd chosen to denote Nature has its obvious pastoral connection with almost everything we understand about Jesus' ministry, but there are other dimensions to the theme of the natural world we inhabit.

We are increasingly aware that we dare not evade our responsibilities relating to environmental issues. The need to conserve energy sources, to reduce, if we can, global warming, to put an end to the spoilation of the rain forests – all are issues which cannot simply be left to 'those who know about such things'. They are matters of urgency for us all, crucial to the survival of our planet and we can, and should, all play our part, however small, in contributing to a safer environment for future generations. We all know ways in which we can change our hitherto selfish habits; we can recycle material and can curb waste, not to mention the influence we could help bring to bear on government departments if we chose to take the time and trouble to do so. And this is a pastoral as well as a social issue (although I think that is a false distinction to make in the majority of situations anyway). If we care about people and about their quality of life we have to be aware of the terrifying possibilities that lie in wait if we fail to heed the warning signs and to act less selfishly in the present decades. When we ask 'who is my neighbour?' we surely cannot respond only in terms of those who happen to belong to our own generation. Our care is for those we shall never know in the future as well as for those we shall never meet in the present.

And it is of people we shall never know in the present that I was reminded by looking at the second light in the window. I doubt whether many of us would choose a warrior nowadays to depict our concept of justice, although the New Testament abounds in pictures of our fighting as soldiers of Christ. But part of 'putting on the whole armour of God' nowadays is surely to fight on the side of those who are oppressed or marginalised, destroyed through poverty or without hope for a number of reasons. The hymn we sang as we turned from the window didn't allow us to escape from our contemporary responsibility –

... For a just and equal sharing
Of the things that earth affords.
To a life of love in action
Help us rise and pledge our word.

All that kills abundant living
Let it from the earth be banned;
Pride of status, race, or schooling,
Dogmas that obscure your plan.
In our common quest for justice
May we hallow life's brief span.

Fred Kaan

Of course we must try to right wrongs which we see on our own doorstep but Leslie Burgin – as have many men and women before and since – took issue with injustice by becoming a Member of Parliament and trying to influence the political and social structure of his day. It is an obligation which rests with all of us to a greater or lesser degree. It is no use singing piously about the quest for justice unless we are prepared to be active participants in that quest. We can't all be MPs, but we can all speak out about integrity in government and about policies which are clearly at variance with our understanding of a God who loves all his children equally and who is always on the side of the least and the lowest.

The figure of mature wisdom holding the book of the law was not as immediately clear to me as a pastoral image but as I thought about it afterwards the parallels seemed numerous. To act responsibly in pastoral matters requires wisdom, it requires understanding and in very many ways it also requires 'sticking to the rules'. Perhaps it would be more helpful to talk about knowing where the limits are and about recognising boundaries. We cannot, for example, infringe another person's privacy in our caring; we have to have the wisdom to know when we must allow someone else – however close to us they may be – to choose for themselves what we may consider to be the wrong path; we have to maintain strict laws of confidentiality. Moreover, there is a law of love which supersedes the sterile legalistic codes which we still allow ourselves to be bound by on occasion and it is a law of love which, by making us accountable and responsible, also frees us to care with wisdom and understanding, whilst helping us to avoid sheer sentimentality and 'doing good' in a spirit of self-righteousness.

The fourth figure of Service was included specifically to commemorate the work that Dr Burgin did in the provision of equal rights for men and women in the matter of divorce and the Guardianship of Infants Bill (1925) by which equal rights were given to both father and mother. Echoes here for us of the kind of service in which so many Christians and those of other faiths are engaged as they struggle with issues of equality and freedom, especially perhaps at present with issues concerning race, gender and disability.

But the word 'service' relates to all that we mean by pastoral ministry. Jesus said, 'I am among you as one who serves.' We who follow in his footsteps are called to a life of ministry and service which is at the heart of our discipleship. But Jesus also said, 'No longer do I call you servants – I have called you friends.' And it is as both servants and friends of our Lord and of each other that we seek to act responsibly in our living out of our Christian faith. We need each other. We need each other's love and support and prayers as we offer our service and our care within the context of our community, our nation and our world; and I believe most of us – and to my shame I include myself in this – need to do far more 'acting' in these areas and far less 'talking about acting'.

Throughout history men and women have been humbled and inspired by those who have been the prophets of their generation, those who have dared to care regardless of the consequences to themselves, who have moved out from the safety of the church to confront the needs and challenges facing human beings in all walks of life. Are we, too, brave enough to grapple with the injustices and inequalities in our present day society so that it more closely resembles God's kingdom? Or do we let our preoccupation with activities within the life of the church or our own homes become a means of escape from the crucial issues which tear society apart and cry out for us to become involved on God's behalf? They are essential questions to ask ourselves both as a Church and as individuals. The crux will be whether we have the courage to listen to the Holy Spirit's prompting in these matters and whether we dare, in God's strength, to act responsibly as part of God's Church in the world in a new and dynamic way.

Ann Bird

For reflection

- Do you think Christians should be involved in party politics?
  Should the Church play a prophetic role in the nation's life?

- Are there limits to our caring for others? If so, how do we
  discover what they should be?

- The answer to the question 'Who is my neighbour?' will be
  different for each of us. Who do you think *your* neighbour is? –
  or should be?

Our task today is recklessness . . . For what we (as a church) lack is
most assuredly not psychology or literature. We lack a holy rage . . .A
holy rage. The recklessness which comes from the knowledge of God
and humanity. The ability to rage when justice lies prostrate on the
streets and when the lie rages across the face of the earth. A holy anger
about things that are wrong in the world. To rage against the ravaging
of God's earth and the destruction of God's world. To rage when little
children must die of hunger while the tables of the rich are sagging with
food. To rage at the senseless killing of so many and against the
madness of militarism. To rage at the lie that calls the threat of death
and the strategy of destruction 'peace'. To rage against the complacency
of so many in the church who fail to see that we shall live only by the
truth, and that our fear will be the death of us all . . . To restlessly seek
that recklessness that will challenge, and to seek to change human
history until it conforms to the norms of the kingdom of God.

Allan Boesak

A church that doesn't provoke any crises,
a gospel that doesn't unsettle,
a word of God that doesn't get under anyone's skin,
a word of God that doesn't touch the real sin
of the society in which it is being proclaimed,
what gospel is that?
Very nice, pious considerations
     that don't bother anyone,
that's the way many would like preaching to be.
Those preachers who avoid every thorny matter
     so as not to be harassed,
     so as not to have conflicts and difficulties,
do not light up the world they live in.
They don't have Peter's courage, who told that crowd
where the bloodstained hands still were
that had killed Christ:
     'You killed him!'
Even though the charge could cost him his life as
well,
     he made it.
The gospel is courageous;
it's the good news
     of him who came to take away the world's sins.

Oscar Romero

102

The Stranger

Why were the Jews so angry with Jesus
that day when he preached
in the Synagogue at Nazareth
that they attempted to kill him?
Was it because he dared to say
he saw the movement of God
in the action of a poor widow
of another race?
It was not the righteous people of God
but the stranger,
from her experience of poverty and famine,
who shared her food.
And he saw God's presence
in the unbelieving Naaman
who came from Syria, another race,
and recognised the true prophet
and asked to be healed.
In Christ,
God himself broke into life,
coming in from outside,
a stranger.

The stranger is rarely welcome;
he sees too clearly
our empty respectable ways,
our narrow vision
and the chains of our religion.
He sides with outcasts
and offends good worthy church folk.
He is always present,
coming from the streets,
the Third World,
from prison,
naked and hungry
piercing our ignorance
with insights
and lessons
from his own bitter experience.

Author unknown

You asked for my hands
that you might use them for your purpose.
I gave them for a moment then withdrew them
for the work was hard.

You asked for my mouth
to speak out against injustice.
I gave you a whisper that I might not be accused.

You asked for my eyes
to see the pain of poverty.
I closed them for I did not want to see.

You asked for my life
that you might work through me.
I gave a small part that I might not get too involved.

Lord, forgive my calculated efforts to serve you,
only when it is convenient for me to do so,
only in those places where it is safe to do so,
and only with those who make it easy to do so.

Father, forgive me,
renew me
send me out
as a usable instrument
that I might take seriously
the meaning of your cross.

Joe Seremane

*Most merciful Father, you have called us to be a caring Church,
reflecting in our lives your infinite care for us your children.*

*Help us to fulfil our calling and to care for one another in an
unselfish fellowship of love; and to care for the world around us in
sharing with it the good news of your love and serving those who
suffer from poverty, hunger and disease.*

We ask it in the name of Christ our Lord.

Michael Ramsey

HAVING FUN

Thank goodness Jesus enjoyed attending and celebrating a wedding, sought out the company of his friends such as Martha and Mary, and allowed his innate sense of humour to sparkle through the parables by which he taught. Thank goodness some of the most attractive saints and prophets have had a good sense of humour like Teresa of Avila or Desmond Tutu. Thank goodness God has created a world for us to live in which is full of colour and beauty, fun and variety; and thank goodness he has made us in such a way that our relationships with each other are intended to include relaxation together and light-hearted fun and happiness.

In the anthology *Flowing Streams* there is a quotation from an unknown source which underlines this:

> God made laughter for himself
> when his children on earth
> took themselves too seriously;
>
> And he gave it to Jesus
> to share with his friends,
> to use in his stories,
> to praise in young children,
> To bring to the sad.
>
> So we dare not, in our wisdom,
> doubt that God inhabits humour,
> nor condemn him to be dour
> like some bankrupt undertaker.
>
> From his spirit issues joy,
> and that fruit is for our healing.

I think we have abundant proof that 'God inhabits humour'. We only have to look at some of the nature programmes on television and watch the antics of the penguins or the incredible shapes of some of the animals he has made, or the courting rituals of some of the more exotic birds, to see it in action. Or, maybe, we only have to look at ourselves to see how foolish we can be when we take ourselves too seriously and to recognise how hard it is to retain a true perspective on life if we don't allow our sense of humour to flourish.

Perhaps the theme suggests itself to me today because as I write this I am about to have a visitation from two of my grandchildren and I know what will happen before they have been in the house for very long. Mark, aged two and a half, will grab my hand and say, 'Come, Gan-gan (his version of granny!), hidey!' and I shall be expected to clamber under a hot duvet and wait there with him, sweltering, in the hope that someone will have noticed that we have disappeared before I die of suffocation! Fun? – of course it is, as is the chance to sit transfixed again watching *Aladdin* ('La-lad'), *Pinnochio* and the *Aristocats*.

'Our spirit can become weary with straining after God, as our body can become weary with overwork,' wrote Richard Foster. I do not need to 'strain after God' when I am with my grandchildren. He is self-evident and not least in the fun we have together. I can become a child again and not in any superficial sense but with a profound gratitude for the trust and love and acceptance that can exist so naturally between us. It reminds me of so much we are in danger of losing with each other as we grow older if we cannot retain the ability to have fun and to deepen our relationships through laughter and celebration.

Children have so much to teach us about fun. They enjoy the moment in all its fullness and concentrate wholeheartedly on what they are about even if it's only for short periods of time. They are also bursting with curiosity and a sense of wonder; they are uninhibited and full of imagination and creativity. My grandchildren have already reminded me simply by example that I need to look at each person as if I were doing it for the first time and that I need to share what exists in each moment as if there were no end to it. And as I write I think how close all that sounds to my understanding of 'the sacrament of the present moment' and wonder how often we connect that phrase with 'having fun'. And if not, why not?

I have, as we all have, a great number of memories of times when life has felt unbearably sad or difficult, but as I look back I find that equally strong are the memories of the times when I have had enormous fun. The list could be endless but two occasions spring to mind in particular, both relating to family occasions.

The first was the hilarious speech our son Peter made at his wedding when he recalled a disastrous family holiday on the Norfolk Broads. The second was one of our wedding anniversaries when the whole family was on holiday in Cornwall together and we were enjoying a celebratory meal. Suddenly my eldest son (then aged about twenty four!) looked across the table at his father and said, 'Dad, I'd never realised you've got such big ears! Do they get bigger as you get older?' – which would have been funny enough in itself (not that it's true, of course!) if it hadn't been compounded by the fact that we were so doubled up with laughter that none of us noticed the waitress approach to take our order until we heard her saying to my husband, 'Can you hear me, sir?' The poor waitress had to come back later – herself helpless with laughter by this time! – and 'Dad's ears' have been the butt of many a family joke since then, especially since the British Medical Journal published an article proving that men's ears do indeed get bigger as they get older!

Taking life too seriously does not make us whole people or good 'carers'. Wallace Stevens wrote some relevant lines on this theme:

> Rationalists, wearing square hats,
> Think, in square rooms,
> Looking at the floor,
> Looking at the ceiling.
> They confine themselves
> To right-angled triangles.
> If they tried rhomboids,
> Cones, waving lines, ellipses –
> As, for example, the ellipse of the half-moon –
> Rationalists would wear sombreros.

I fancy the idea of approaching life wearing a sombrero! I believe in hard work, commitment, involvement – the demands laid upon us by our call to be God's serving, caring people. But I also believe in sitting lightly enough to life to be fully receptive to the wonder and joy and fun of it all. Jurgen Moltmann said, 'Where freedom of play has been lost, the world turns into a desert', and the world, as we have allowed it to become, is desert enough without our making it worse by making it over-serious.

Those who belong to the long line of 'Holy Fools' – clowns within the Christian Church – know the truth of this and it is a truth we all need to recognise as carers, not just as carers of other people but as carers of ourselves.

Bill Peckham, who founded the 'Holy Fools in America' movement, vouches for people's desire to have fun as a major need – as a kind of 'skin hunger':

> It's almost the same kind of hunger that we experience for food or liquid. And it's true, people are dying not because of physical ailments but because of skin hunger. I think one of the main duties of the religious clown is to help meet this skin hunger, to bring in love, affection, touch, maybe to entertain, to bring a smile where there was no smile. The stories are almost legion where a clown has come into a room with a person who has not spoken for five years and had that person speak, or dealt with someone who hadn't laughed for months and months and had that person break into a guffaw that just brings down that corner of the hospital. As far as I'm concerned that is clowning to me. Maybe laughter is one of the most religious experiences to have, not when it's laughter at the expense of someone else but just heart-warming laughter because you're enjoying life, and the clown is helping you to enjoy it all the more.

If that is part of the ministry of the clown it is a ministry vital to all of us who want to help people discover an oasis in their desert experience and who want to celebrate the knowledge that life is meant to be enjoyed. We have, wherever possible, to affirm that God delights in his creation and that if we can stand in God's kingdom like a child on tiptoe, wide-eyed with astonishment at the glorious unexpectedness and humour of it all, we shall experience the deep holiness of 'having fun'.

Ann Bird

The people in your house group or on your visiting list will not be anything like this, of course, but think how you would try to care for each individual if they were!

For reflection

What would you like to have done that you haven't? Is it too late? If so, what else can you do instead?

- What is your understanding of 'the sacrament of the present moment'?

- Think about times of fun and laughter that you have experienced.

If I had my life to live over again,
I'd try to make more mistakes next time:
I would relax, I would limber up,
    I would be sillier than I have been this trip.
I know of very few things I would take seriously.
I would take more trips, I would be crazier . . .
I would eat more ice cream and less beans
I would have more actual troubles and fewer imaginary ones.
You see I'm one of those people who lives life
    sensibly hour after hour, day after day.
Oh, I've had my moments, and if I had
    to do it over again, I'd have more of them . . .

Tim Hansel

A holiday from myself

I don't think I'll be able to have a proper holiday this year; I'll only be able to have bits of holiday as opportunities arise.

But this morning I gave myself a lovely bit: I decided I was going to give myself a holiday from myself. For one whole morning I wouldn't let myself be bullied by that voice within me which makes me feel guilty about everything I do and mucks me up.

You know the sort of thing. Just as you are about to crash into a slice of toast and marmalade (with marge, not even butter) that awful inner voice starts to go on and on about duty and charity, and though you eat the toast because it would be wasteful and useless not to, the voice takes the joy out of the marmalade and puts the guilt on to the gingerbread.

I'm also going to give myself a holiday from horrors. Yes, I might have leprosy, housemaid's knee, piles and the plague and don't know it, but until 12.45 pm I'm not even going to think of it. And that goes for the Bomb as well. I shan't protest or demonstrate until I've had the longest soak in the fullest bath, foaming with a few pennorth of 'orchid' detergent I splashed out on at the supermarket.

I am also not going to dress, but wander round the house in my oldest, most threadbare and comfortable bathrobe, which I didn't even buy but inherited. (It came from Harrods in 1936.) And if anyone knocks, who cares! They'll have to lose their ecclesiastical illusions. After all, religion isn't a dry-cleaned suit with deodorant and dentures. I don't know what the prophets looked like, but I suspect they were kitted out in old bathrobes like me and never used after-shave, if they ever shaved at all.

I'm also going to enjoy some religion – yes, I mean enjoy it! I am going to lie on the floor and listen to the lush bits of *Elijah* on the gramophone, with plummy voices backed up by lashings of strings and brass. I don't care if my inner voice agonises as to whether it is kitsch or culture. I enjoy it in a damp sort of way, because the vibrato turns on my tear-ducts. In the sad parts I shall allow myself to moan with the horns.

I am not going to be persuaded into thinking about my prospects – and that includes pension (if any), wardened flats, retirement homes, and jolly geriatric trips to the seaside (out of season). I shall read adverts for hair replacement instead, which always makes me think more hopefully and happily about our moans and hormones.

I shall read comforting religious thoughts in homey magazines and look through DIY journals to find out how to make a bedsitter 'regency' at minimal cost.

I shall do all the things my inner voice disapproves of. I shall chat on the telephone, while sitting in the bath. I shall eat cold custard straight from the tin (not sitting in the bath). I shall plan dinner parties I'll never give. I shall concentrate on my favourite childhood game: 'If a witch gave you three wishes what would you wish . . ?'

Until 12.45 pm I am going to love myself as my neighbour. I shall keep eleven commandments, not just ten – I shall not commit myself!

Lionel Blue

There is, it sometimes seems, an excess of religious and social business these days, a round of committees and conferences and journeyings, of which the cost in 'peaceable wisdom' is not sufficiently counted. Sometimes we appear overmuch to count as merit our participation in these things . . . At least we ought to make sure that we sacrifice our leisure for something worthy. True leisureliness is a beautiful thing and may not lightly be given away. Indeed, it is one of the outstanding and most wonderful features of the life of Christ that, with all his work in preaching and healing and planning for the Kingdom, he leaves behind this sense of leisure, of time in which to pray and meditate, to stand and stare at the cornfields and fishing boats and to listen to the confidences of neighbours and passers-by . . .

Most of us need from time to time the experience of something spacious or space-making, when Time ceases to be the enemy, goad-in-hand, and becomes our friend. To read good literature, gaze on natural beauty, to follow cultivated pursuits until our spirits are refreshed and expanded, will not unfit us for the up and doing of life, whether of personal or church affairs. Rather will it help us to separate the essential from the unessential, to know where we are really needed and get a sense of proportion. We shall find ourselves giving the effect of leisure even in the midst of a full and busy life. People do not pour their joys or sorrows into the ears of those with an eye on the clock.

Caroline C Graveson

111

Dear Lord, I thank you for calling me to share with others your precious gift of laughter. May I never forget that it is your gift and my privilege. As your children are rebuked in their self-importance and cheered in their sadness, help me to remember that your foolishness is wiser than men's wisdom.

The Clown's Prayer (Source unknown)

* * * *

Give me a sense of humour, Lord, and also things to laugh about, give me the grace to take a joke against myself and to see the funny side of the things I do; save me from annoyance, bad temper, resentfulness against my friends. Help me to laugh even in the face of trouble, fill my mind with the love of Jesus; for his name's sake. Amen.

Michael Hollings and Etta Gullick

* * * *

O God, the source of the whole world's gladness and bearer of its pain, may your unconquerable joy rest at the heart of all our trouble and distress, through Jesus Christ our Lord, Amen.

* * * *

Be still and know that I am God.

Psalm 46: 10

Loving God, I thank you for all the lovely things of life. Help me to recognise them and enjoy them to the full. Amen.

TRACING THE RAINBOW

1. STRANDS OF HOPE

O joy that seekest me through pain,
I cannot close my heart to thee:
I trace the rainbow through the rain,
And feel the promise is not vain,
That morn shall tearless be.

This verse is from a hymn written by George Matheson, who has described the circumstances of its composition in the following words:

It was composed with extreme rapidity: it seemed to me that its construction occupied only a few minutes, and I felt myself rather in the position of one who was being dictated to than of an original artist. I was suffering from extreme mental distress, and the hymn was the fruit of pain.

As it was for George Matheson, so it is frequently true for us that our most intuitive, deep, and even positive responses to life occur precisely at those times when our circumstances are particularly difficult or sad. We become conscious that everything about us appears to be more sharply defined and detailed, that there is a greater clarity about the created world we inhabit and that all our senses seem heightened and intensified. Experiences of such significance often remain deeply imprinted on our memory and in any event will almost certainly have a lasting effect on us.

My own memories of past happenings are notoriously elusive! I live very much in the present and am frequently surprised by accounts of events at which I was obviously present and of which I have no recollection whatsoever. And yet the painful landmark experiences stand out in stark detail – as do the precious occasions of unmitigated joy – and it seems that in relation to such times I remember everything I did, everything that was said, everything that affected me in any way.

It is worth taking time to reflect on these landmark experiences for sometimes when we are in the midst of them we have energy only for survival; reflection and contemplation are beyond us.

One of the exercises used in pastoral care workshops is to suggest that people draw their own 'life-lines', asking them to chart their 'good' times above the line and the 'not-so-good' or 'bad' ones below the line. After a period of sharing together about these 'life-lines' it seems to be the general consensus of opinion not only that the 'bad' times impinge more markedly upon us but that, in retrospect, we have all experienced our greatest inner growth as a result of such times.

That is not to say that the path of bereavement, redundancy, illness, or of whatever life has dealt in terms of personal hardship is not real or sharply felt. We are human and we hurt. We grieve and we cry out in anger and bewilderment at our helplessness and at the apparent injustice of it all. And yet, if we have begun to learn the healing power of 'tracing the rainbow' at such times, we find that in some mysterious way, as life moves on, our hurt and our pain have been transformed into what looks strangely like gain.

But this does not happen of its own accord. We have to allow ourselves to be open enough to all our experiences for them to enter us deeply. We have to accept them realistically and we have to accept that all that we can do with them is to try to find what is God's will for us within what is happening to us. And as we begin to live in this way we discover that 'rainbow'glimpses may come along the way through the support of friends, through unexpected moments of humour even in the darkest circumstances, through music heard or a word spoken or read – all are intimations of the grace of God with us and signs of his continuing love and graciousness towards us 'at all times and in all places'.

And it is at *all* times and in *all* places, too, that we are to give thanks to God – though that is easier said than done. It is far less challenging to rail against life and its hurtfulness than to seek meaning and occasion for gratitude. Yet to be able to give thanks, to find blessing in all things, is a mark of Christian living. Thankfulness is the prism through which the colours of the rainbow can be glimpsed even when life is at its darkest and most unwelcoming.

For most of us, though, the majority of our life is lived at a comparatively mundane level. We face 'rain' rather than 'storm'. But if we cultivate a thankful approach to life in its ordinary ups and downs, in the normal 'rainy' seasons, we are preparing the ground for when thankfulness is farthest from our thoughts.

It is about trying to see the lovely, the hopeful, the positive and gracious in every situation. It is about looking for the colour and light and vitality in life rather than dwelling on the drab and pessimistic and life-denying side of existence. And it is about recognising, too, that we are not always going to be successful in our attempts and that to see life in this perspective is a great deal harder for some of us than for others, depending on our circumstances, or our temperament, or our relationships at any given time.

As you read now, pause to make a mental list of your own 'rainbow' moments during the last week, in the recent past. Such moments may be concerned with our own individual experience or with hopeful signs in the wider life of community, or of international politics, but wherever their focus they are worth remembering and savouring and weaving strands of colour and hopefulness into our individual tapestry of experience. Indeed, the more sombre the general pattern may be for us the more brightly do the coloured strands stand out in relief as contrast and promise.

In his original version of the verse quoted at the beginning, George Matheson wrote, 'I *climb* the rainbow through the rain' and for most of us the image of climbing seems a particularly apt metaphor to describe our struggle to cope in the dark experiences of life. We cling on to our faith in the face of all the evidence, believing that the rainbow we glimpse ahead of us is not just an illusion to tantalise and disappoint us but a promise of God's presence with us as it was to the people of Israel, a sign of God's love and blessing over-arching all that is before us.

And what encourages so many of us to go on 'climbing' with confidence is our knowledge that the rainbow's promise has been fulfilled again and again in our own experience.

Ann Bird

May faith in God uphold you
may the hope of God overarch you
may the love of God surround you.

Light of the world:
through our tears of sorrow
our tears of joy
our shared tears
we see refracted
the many colours of your creation
the mingled colours of your promise:

Jan S Pickard

116

For reflection

- During a time of quietness draw your own 'life-line' as suggested. Then share with a friend the memory of a particular time when you learnt the healing power of tracing the rainbow in difficult circumstances.

- What lifts your spirit?

- 'Pray to God in the storm but keep on rowing!' Does this Danish proverb hold truth for you?

Walking on water looks difficult,
but I have seen it done.

Those with enough grief to sink them
have kept on –
drawn by an invisible
source of strength
they were not let down.

Crossing this sea
some swim
and others drown,
but some there are
walking on water.

Cecily Taylor

* * * *

Loving Father, give me enough faith to 'walk on water' and to give you thanks whatever my circumstances. Amen.

2. THE COLOUR OF FREEDOM

I intended to begin by quoting a verse from the song which inspired the title for John McCarthy and Jill Morrell's account of his time as a hostage and her attempts to have him released. Unfortunately the complexities of copyright defeated me! But if you have read *Some Other Rainbow* you will have seen the poem at the beginning which speaks of the hopelessness experienced by all those left 'waiting in the cold' while others, for one reason or another, have gone away 'clinging to some other rainbow' and leaving them bereft. For John and Jill, 'some other rainbow' suggested the ever-widening distance that can separate those who have freedom and choice from those who are trapped in situations of loneliness or deprivation or fear. It spoke of the way in which those who are free to do so tend to 'cling to rainbows', seeking to maintain their own security and comfort often at the expense of those who are left out in the cold, fobbed off with false promises and a general lack of concern.

Very few people know the experience of being a hostage like John McCarthy, but many, many people in the world are 'waiting in the cold' in one way or another. It is on their behalf that, as carers within the Church, we should be seeking for freedom and for justice.

It is all too easy to agree with the statement that the Church should care about social and political issues and that 'something' should be done, without being prepared to take the Church's prophetic role upon oneself and campaign vigorously for change and greater compassion in at least one aspect of the issues at stake. On some topics the Church is united enough to speak with one voice within the nation or community and on some occasions its voice is heard and acted upon so that somewhere, for some people, the quality of life improves to a greater or lesser extent. That is always good and always something we should be striving towards. But Jill Morrell fought a comparatively lonely battle on behalf of someone for whom she cared deeply and for a cause that she believed to be right until more and more people became convinced that something positive must be done and John was freed.

Of course, in that particular situation, there were several other factors involved in the freeing of the hostages, but probably most moves for good are the result of a complexity of pressures and events. It is nevertheless true that frequently the original impetus for our committed action to a particular cause is that we have known someone who has suffered some particular ill-treatment or injustice or we have been caught up in a community where specific hardship is taking its toll of people's lives. Once our compassionate imagination is caught and held we are far more likely to engage fully with the problems that need to be tackled and remain actively involved for as long as it takes for change to occur.

The trouble is that we are surrounded by so many needs and demands that we feel overwhelmed by our own apparent inadequacy for making any difference in any direction at all, or we become discouraged because any effort we do make often seems ineffectual and frighteningly unimportant in the face of the massive problem. But not being able to do much is no excuse for doing nothing! The kingdom of heaven can grow from a grain of mustard seed. We are not actually asked to do more than we can cope with. We are, after all, members of the Body of Christ; we do not have to take everything upon ourselves and no one of us can ever become involved with more than a tiny fraction of the need we see around us. Each person has their particular contribution to make and we all have to examine our conscience to discover what kind of involvement God is asking from us.

Most of us would not claim that we have got the balance right. The sorting out of priorities is notoriously difficult, but we only have to read Matthew 25 to know that we have to make some kind of prayerful decisions about such priorities and then act upon them. It is unrealistic to think that we can take an intelligent interest in every international trouble-spot in the world to the point where we can lobby government, be supportive of particular people or agencies working to alleviate the situation, and pray with detailed knowledge as well as with loving concern.

We can, however, choose to identify ourselves with one country in particular – South Africa, Bosnia, Northern Ireland, El Salvador – and make that the focus of our prayers and study and active support. Similarly, as citizens we are aware that caring agencies – the Samaritans, the Terence Higgins Trust, the hospice movement, Shelter, the Institute for Race Relations – need all the financial help and practical support they can command, but we have to limit ourselves as individuals to the one or two which seem most appropriate for us.

Even when we think about our caring for individuals we know that there is a limit to how many people 'waiting in the cold' we can truly befriend so that we enter into a worthwhile relationship of any depth with them. Practical acts of kindness and friendship, shared times of crisis, are part and parcel of everyday living and we respond as each occasion requires. But an ongoing commitment to a particular individual or group is far more time-consuming, and by our choice of that person or group as a priority we are inevitably excluding others who would also welcome a considerable amount of our time and energy.

It is still true, though, that the one thing we cannot afford to do is to allow ourselves to be so overwhelmed by all the possibilities that we opt for the easy way of staying on the sidelines and not taking part in the action at all. Those who are fortunate enough to enjoy in varying measure freedom, peace of mind, friendship, security, health, dignity – some of the rainbow colours of life that enhance even the dark times and make them more bearable – are quite unequivocally called by God to share in other people's pain and frustration and brokenness and to alleviate it wherever possible.

We are required to bridge gaps and heal divisions and to enable people to see signs of colour and hope in life so that their own lives are transformed as a rainbow transforms the sky after a storm. The clouds are still there, the traces of rain are still evident and yet the rainbow is the dominant feature in the scene as a whole.

D H Lawrence's novel *The Rainbow* ends with Ursula Brangwen's vision of a rainbow at a point where everything else in life seemed to have fragmented and failed. She was aware of 'a rainbow forming itself. In one place it gleamed fiercely, and, her heart anguished with hope, she sought the shadow of iris where the bow should be. Steadily the colour gathered, mysteriously, from nowhere, it took presence upon itself, there was a faint, vast rainbow. The arc bended and strengthened itself till it arched indomitable, making great architecture of light and colour and the space of heaven, its pedestals luminous in the corruption of new houses on the low hill, its arch the top of heaven. And the rainbow stood on the earth.'

We have to begin from where people are. We have to 'stand on the earth'. We have to do all in our power to create a world and a society and a community where there is hope and freedom and justice and where everyone's life is touched with the promise of God and the knowledge of his overarching love.

It is not 'some other rainbow', different for different people and more visible to some than to others that we ultimately want to see. It is

the same rainbow common to all so that all can see in it as Ursula did –
'the earth's new architecture . . . the world built up in a living fabric of
truth, fitting to the over-arching heaven'.

Ann Bird

- Do you feel overwhelmed by 'compassion fatigue?' In the face
  of all the world's needs and demands how do you establish
  your own priorities for caring or giving?

- 'Freedom' means much more than the opportunity to do what
  we like or go where we want. What do you understand by the
  word 'freedom'?

- 'Love your neighbour as yourself.' How readily do you accept
  the second part of Jesus' commandment and in what ways do
  you love yourself?

Again I've seen
Into 'the world of difference'.

She came in grey thin pieces of cloth
With two children at her side,
Shadows of people;
Pinched old faces
In children's bodies;
Big eyes
– no anger
– no resentment
At our health and plenty;
– just tired acceptance.
Perhaps our eyes echoed
The anger for them!
Stunted growth with thin spindly legs
Tried to balance on the scales,
Wobbling like a new-born foal.

This time no car window
Between us
– that other world was standing before me
In bones and flesh.
Food, clothing,
Love and care were prescribed.

Lord,
Is this You standing here?
Is this the opportunity given
To feed and clothe You?
Do I hear You say
'When you do it for the least of these
my children you do it for Me!'?

Alison Stedman

* * * *

God of compassion, may we be among those who are working for
freedom and justice for all who are 'waiting in the cold' in our world
today. Amen.

The restless clouds,
Ever-moving
ride across the sky
or creep down
to sit in the lap of the mountains.

In bright sunshine
like icing-sugar crowns
they cover the peaks.

In dull wet drizzle
they hang . . .
like cobwebs
in the corners of the mountains;
curtaining the valley
to its eerie rain-filled fate.

So lace fine
you can't capture or touch
their delicateness.
Pearl misty droplets
escape your fingers
. . . and disintegrate;
leaving cold dampness
on hair and skin
like the trace of a dewy morning.

Then
there is nothing so beautiful
so magical
so distant or fleeting,
as a rainbow's painted colours
brushed across the whiteness
with a master stroke
from the promise-remembering
Creator!

Alison Stedman

3. RAINBOW COLOURS CAUGHT UP IN THE SUN

> I see you
> a rainbow
> painted in the sky
> of my own life,
> an orchestra of stars
> whose music
> rises in the wind and storm
> and echoes
> in the mountain peaks.

When I first read this poem by Margaret Torrie, founder of CRUSE, I sat for a long while applying its imagery to the people who mean most to me. Family and friends rested in my mind's eye one by one as I took time to recognise and acknowledge the particular gifts and graces that each one brings to the relationships we have with each other.

I found that the picture of the rainbow stressed how individual each person is, the rainbow colours reflecting the differences in personality and temperament, all of which are there to be treasured and enjoyed. It reminded me, too, that I have to be more accepting of such differences than I often am.

It is no use my expecting someone at one end of the temperamental spectrum to be able to behave like someone at the opposite end just because it would make life more comfortable for me. Neither should I expect introverts suddenly to become extroverts or people with strong opinions and likes and dislikes suddenly to become muted, indecisive characters who want always to fade into the background. We are created to be different, and as the colours of the rainbow are especially vivid because they have their own definition in contrast to each other, so, as people, our differences complement each other and highlight our unique value.

Nowhere is this more so than in our differences of colour and race, which was once perfectly expressed in the 'Prayer for the Day' on Radio 4 chosen by Itemeleng Mosala:

God, some people are saying that you are colour blind;
that you don't care whether a person is black or white,
or any other colour,
and so we shouldn't care either.

Well, I can't accept that.
People are important.
Their eyes are important
Their names are important
Their race is important
And their colour is important.
Colour is good, Lord,
It's full of life.
I have a hunch that Adam was black,
Eve was white,
And Cain was yellow.
And you were all the colours of the rainbow then.
Lord, don't let me ever forget the importance
of every little difference between me and my brother,
me and my parents,
me and my maker,
and teach me to honour them
just the way they are.
Then I will be proud to be
The way you made me. Amen.

It would be wrong to stretch the imagery of Margaret Torrie's poem too far. Each person will respond to the poem in their own way, but its ability to help me reflect on the loveliness and strength-giving nature of our friendships was reinforced by the lines which speak of 'an orchestra of stars/whose music/rises in the wind and storm'. Friendship is surely at its most apparent when the going is rough and we realise again how blessed we are in those who care enough about us to be in tune with our needs and with the changing circumstances of our life. The friends I most value are those who seem able to accept me for who I am, forgive me for what I cannot be and who appear to enjoy my company in spite of all my failings. They are those, too, who have been there when I have most needed their support and affection and who have seemed on occasion to understand me better than I understand myself.

I warm to the lines about friendship that I wrote down many years ago, although I have no idea who the author is:

> Permit your friends to be themselves. Accept them as they are. Be grateful for what is there, not annoyed by what friends cannot give. Accept each one's imperfections and individuality, and don't feel threatened if their opinions and tastes differ from yours.
>
> Give praise and encouragement. Tell your friends what you like about them, how thankful you are for their presence in your life. Delight in their talents, applaud their successes.

Friendship both happens to us and is perpetuated by us. So often we assume that once we have acquired friends they will care for us, or at least put up with us, regardless of the way in which we take them for granted or fail to show our concern for them. Paul wrote to the Colossians: 'Clothe yourselves with compassion, kindness, humility, gentleness and patience. Bear with each other . . .' To have friends who are available for us in this way, who will 'bear with us', is an immense cause for gratitude, but we, too, must be for them 'a rainbow painted in the sky of their own life', offering our thankfulness for them and allowing them to be truly themselves in our relationship with them.

The possibility of experiencing friendship of this depth is there for all of us. We have to learn to listen to our lives and to the lives of others and see them for the vast and deep mysteries that they are. We have to immerse ourselves in the pain and boredom and disillusionment of life as much as we do in the excitement and gladness and hope. In the words of Buechner we have to 'touch, taste and smell our way to the holy and hidden heart of it all because in the last analysis all moments are key moments and all relationships are key relationships, and life itself is grace'.

Awareness of grace is also one of the keys to Christian living and it is a gift of the Spirit which comes to us in precious, unexpected ways. It seems that rainbows, too, are connected with the unexpected. They appear suddenly on the horizon and make our spirits lift. – As Wordsworth wrote:

> My heart leaps up when I behold
> A rainbow in the sky . . .

In ordinary life the unexpected 'rainbow' moments are very special. We hear of some kindness done, enjoy an occasion of fun and laughter, find moments of peace in the midst of a busy life, catch the look on a child's face, visit an old person and come away humbled and grateful for a glimpse of their serenity and courage. But such moments do not last any more than rainbows last and once we have 'traced the rainbow' we have to be prepared to let it go without losing the momentary glory it brought with it.

In her poem 'Elixir' Ann Lewin writes:

> It's not bad weather, only rain.
> Philosophers once thought
> Drops cupped in Lady's Mantle
> Would become pure gold.
> So our imagination can transform
> Grey to a shade of silver, and see
> Rainbow colours caught up in the sun.

That ability to 'see rainbow colours caught up in the sun' is itself a mark of grace. It is an indication that we have begun to recognise the eternal love and friendship of God reflected in our human relationships in many different ways, transforming them and filling them with hope and love and with unlimited potential for good and for delight.

Ann Bird

- What are the qualities you most value in your friends?

- Look again at the prayer chosen by Itemeleng Mosala. What differences between ourselves and others do you find hard to accept? Ability? Culture? Theological understanding? How can you become less prejudiced?

- Write a prayer for your friends.

Grace strikes us when we are in great pain and restlessness. It strikes us when we walk through the dark valley of a meaningless and empty life. Sometimes at that moment a wave of light breaks into our darkness, and it is as though a voice were saying, 'You are accepted. You are accepted, accepted by that which is greater than you, and the name of which you do not know. Do not seek for anything, do not perform anything, do not intend anything. Simply accept the fact that you are accepted.'

Paul Tillich

* * * *

Lord, forgive us the hatreds and prejudices and malice which pull the rug from under all our so-called love for others and for you. Black and White, Catholic and Protestant, Jew and Arab, Croat, Muslim and Serb – so many peoples feed on hatred for one another, endlessly suppressing the truth of our common humanity.

Lord, give courage and compassion, a liberation of the spirit, an opening of heart and mind, so that those thought of only as aliens and enemies may become simply people.

We make our prayer through the Friend of sinners, Jesus Christ our Lord.

Christopher Lamb

* * * *

May the God of love, who is the source of all our affection for each other formed here on earth, take our friendships into his keeping, that they may continue and increase throughout life and beyond it, in Jesus Christ our Lord. Amen.

William Temple

4. THE RAINBOW PEOPLE OF GOD

> God gave us the radiant rainbow
> The splendour and spectrum of love.
> The message of Covenant mercy
> The olive leaf borne by the dove.
> *(Source unknown)*

The God of Israel was often depicted as a warrior god, especially in his role as god of the storm. Psalms 17 and 18 speak of lightning bolts as his arrows which he shoots from his bow. The writer of the Wisdom of Solomon is even more specific: 'Shafts of lightning will fly with true aim, and will leap from the clouds to the target, as from a well-drawn bow . . . '

Yet in the Genesis story the rainbow after the flood is a sign that the God of the storm shall never again use his most powerful weapon for such destruction. He has put it in the clouds as if in storage and the bow's visible presence in the clouds is a guarantee that it is not being used.

> God said, 'This is the sign of the covenant that I make between me and you and every living creature that is with you, for all future generations: I have set my bow in the clouds, and it shall be a sign of the covenant between me and the earth. When I bring clouds over the earth and the bow is seen in the clouds, I will remember my covenant that is between me and you and every living creature of all flesh; and the waters shall never again become a flood to destroy all flesh. When the bow is in the clouds, I will see it and remember the everlasting covenant between God and every living creature of all flesh that is on the earth.'
>
> *Genesis 9: 12-17*

And so the message of covenant mercy was proclaimed even in the Old Testament, a promise and sign of God's unfailing love for us and for all creation. Consequently, in the context of our pastoral ministry, it is tempting to relate the rainbow of the covenant only to the overtly gentle and compassionate aspects of our caring, and to forget that there is still the other dimension which is significantly relevant.

Not that we are concerned about arrows of retribution, for God's justice is always tempered with mercy in his dealings with human beings, but we *are* concerned with the arrows that fly straight to the mark of situations and happenings that are unjust or cruel or contrary to God's will. So often the most practical way in which we can become part of God's pastoral purpose in today's world is by taking issue with all that is dark and 'stormy' for individuals and societies and by trying to effect enough change for the rainbow colours of peace and hope and justice to become visible.

We are called to be 'warriors' ourselves in terms of trying to eradicate social ills such as poverty or disease or homelessness and we are charged as Christian carers with a responsibility to confront and challenge situations and policies which are clearly wrong. It can be a difficult path to tread. Anger and determination have their rightful place in some of our campaigning and yet we must never trample on the dignity and freedom of individuals or treat them with less than courtesy or respect. We need to proceed with wisdom and kindness in all we undertake.

In the iconography of the Greek Orthodox Church the rainbow is one of the symbols of divine wisdom which expresses the beauty of the unity of the whole creation whose centre is Christ. Yet, as we try to align ourselves with God's purpose for ourselves and for others, our own wisdom is often sadly lacking. All too frequently we see events and people in very limited perspective and we respond to situations of crisis or complexity with little thought about the consequences of our action. We rely too much on our own strength and wisdom and fail to centre ourselves through prayer and stillness on the loving wisdom of God.

Listening to God and listening in every way possible to those with whom we are pastorally involved is absolutely essential. Whatever the pastoral situation may be the need is always the same. To the best of our ability we should listen to all that is said and much that is unsaid, and we should see all that is obvious and as much as it is possible for us to perceive beneath the surface. Then, and only then, if any other action than the action of listening is necessary, are we in a position to act.

It is a commonplace to say that listening in all its aspects is at the heart of all our pastoral ministry yet it is only as we listen to God and listen to others that the divine wisdom of the loving God in any way colours our own imagination and judgement and is reflected in all that we do or say.

When we look at an actual rainbow we are seeing white light split up into all its component colours by the small droplets of rain which act as prisms. And as we look at a 'rainbow' as a visual aid for our caring understanding we can let our imagination play with the colour symbolism within it.

There is the colour symbolism understood by Greek iconographers, such as red signifying our humanity and blue signifying the love of God, orange standing for revolution and change, green standing for new life and yellow for eternal life. Or we can look at the liturgical meanings of some of the colours where purple symbolises suffering and green is worn on the 'ordinary' occasions of the Church's year. We can let our minds dwell on the moods we associate with colour – when we feel 'blue' or depressed or 'red' with anger; we can remember the 'jaundiced' outlook we can have on life, or the cowardice and fear associated with yellow. We can also call to mind that in the Book of Revelation the throne of God itself is surrounded by a rainbow.

And as we meditate on the rainbow with all its colours and bring all the symbolic meaning they embody into our pastoral prayers we can remember, too, the words of Desmond Tutu as he introduced Nelson Mandela to the new, democratically elected parliament in South Africa: 'This is the day of liberation for all of us – the rainbow people of God.'

We are indeed all of us, the carers and the cared for and those who are as yet uncared for, the rainbow people of God and we all stand in need of God's message of liberation and mercy and his promise of covenant love. To respond to that unchanging covenant ourselves and to share its loving message with others in every way possible is a privilege and a challenge and a joy. It is the pastoral calling of us all.

Ann Bird

- Are you aware of injustices or needs in your local community? Is there any way in which you can become involved so that at least one situation improves?

- As you think back over the past week, do you feel as though you have 'heard' God in the midst of your daily life? How does he speak to you?

- The rainbow is a sign of hope. Draw a diagram representing the seven curves of a rainbow. In each curve write down something which you see as a sign of hope.

Brothers and sisters in creation, we covenant this day with you and with all creation yet to be;

With every living creature and all that contains and sustains you
With all that is on earth and with the earth itself.
With all that lives in the waters and with the waters themselves
With all that flies in the skies and with the sky itself. We establish this covenant that all our powers will be used to prevent your destruction.

We confess that it is our own kind who put you to death.
We ask for your trust
and as a symbol of our intention
we mark our covenant with you by the rainbow.

This is a sign of the covenant between ourselves
and every living thing that is found on the earth.

*International consultancy on religion,
education and culture.*

* * * *

Glorious God, transform our dullness with the colours of your love and help us to bring brightness to the dark places of the world through hope. Amen.

5. AN EPILOGUE

On the day when my fourth article in the 'Tracing the Rainbow' series appeared in the *Methodist Recorder* my dearly loved mother died. It would be inappropriate here even to try to express how much she meant to me other than to say that she of all the people I have ever known was a shining example of someone who 'traced the rainbow' with joy and love and graciousness through a life which she affirmed as happy but which to others appeared searingly marked by bereavement and ill-health. What I believe *is* appropriate is for me to share two of the 'rainbow' insights I gained as a direct result of her death.

But first, a reminder of the first article which was based on the verse from George Matheson's hymn:

> O joy that seekest me through pain,
> I cannot close my heart to thee:
> I trace the rainbow through the rain,
> And feel the promise is not vain,
> That morn shall tearless be.

One of the exercises frequently used in pastoral care workshops is to suggest that people draw their own 'life-lines', asking them to chart their 'good' times above the line and the 'not-so-good' or 'bad' ones below the line. After a time of sharing together about these 'life-lines' it seems always to be the general consensus of opinion not only that the 'bad' times impinge more markedly upon us but that, in retrospect, we have all experienced our greatest inner growth as a result of such times. That is not to say that the pain of bereavement, redundancy, illness, or of whatever life has dealt in terms of personal hardship is not real or sharply felt. We are human and we hurt. We grieve and we cry out in anger and bewilderment at our helplessness and at the apparent injustice of it all. And yet, if we have begun to learn the healing power of 'tracing the rainbow' at such times, we find that in some mysterious way, as life moves on, our hurt and our pain have been transformed into what looks strangely like gain.

But this does not happen of its own accord. We have to allow ourselves to be open enough to all our experiences for them to enter us deeply. We have to accept them realistically and we have to accept that all that we can do with them is to try to find what is God's will for us within what is happening to us. And as we begin to live in this way we discover that 'rainbow' glimpses may come along the way through the support of friends, through unexpected moments of humour even in the darkest circumstances; through music heard or a word spoken or read – all are intimations of the grace of God with us and signs of his continuing love and graciousness towards us 'at all times and in all places'.

What follows will not be an echo in miniature of C S Lewis' moving book *A Grief Observed*. Nor do I have any easy remedies for circumnavigating the normal process of grieving even if I wanted to discover some. When we love deeply we inevitably experience deep hurt and loss when the person we love dies. In a sense our grief is part of what we still have to give to them and what we need to experience fully for our own eventual healing. So I still believe, in the midst of my own present pain and my struggle to cope with all the changes bereavement brings, that it is only by going directly into the storm of it all that we discern the rainbow signs and the creative, positive face of grief which can be visible to us all.

My mother at the end suffered a massive stroke. She was already nearly blind, coping with unstable diabetes, heart and thyroid problems, severe arthritis and, latterly, a strange swelling of her body which no-one could really explain. Through all this and for many years she had been uncomplaining and full of zest for life and concern for other people. So as I sat with her while she was dying and whilst we could apparently no longer communicate I found myself giving thanks repeatedly not just for her life and all she had meant to me but also for the fact that I could honestly say I had no regrets about our relationship with each other. I sat beside her thinking how desperate I would be feeling if I were to be loaded with guilt or sadness about things left undone or unspoken as well as torn apart by the knowledge of impending parting. At the time such thoughts were strengthening and it was a measure of the lovely, forgiving and gracious person she was that I was able to feel so at peace about the lifetime of love and friendship we had shared.

But after her death, I felt profoundly challenged by my 'no regrets' attitude. I do not need anyone else's illness or death to remind me that I frequently fall short of being the wife, mother, friend or colleague that I am capable of being if I could only find it in myself to be the light-hearted, welcoming, non-judgemental, unselfish person I want in my best moments to be – and which so often proves to be an unattainable mirage! So I am challenged to look again at my relationship with those with whom I *can* still communicate and to resolve once again to try to live more creatively within the sacrament of each present moment, resting in God's grace and knowing that forgiveness and understanding are gifts to be given and received in all circumstances of life. 'No regrets' probably itself seems like an unattainable mirage in most of our ongoing encounters with each other but my mother's death certainly put the rest of my life in perspective. It is no use waiting until it is too late to try to build bridges or to treat people lovingly. We have to try to sort out our relationships here and now while we still have the opportunity.

St Benedict instructed the monks and nuns of his order to say the Lord's Prayer to each other at least twice a day because as they did so they would be required to forgive each other before injuries and hurts could throw up insuperable barriers or damage relationships. Minor irritations and grievances do not normally stretch our powers of forgiveness too far but perhaps one of the most fundamental lessons we are called upon to learn in life is to forgive each other for not being perfect. If we can cultivate that attitude along the way we will almost certainly find the deeper hurts and injustices that come our way more manageable and we shall want to make our peace with each other as a natural way of life. Then, in the final analysis, 'no regrets' can become a positive affirmation of the joys and sorrows experienced together by imperfect loving people who have looked always for the good and lovely in one another.

The second insight and challenge came as I read an extract in the CRUSE anthology, *All In The End Is Harvest*. As a rainbow illuminates the sky unexpectedly and its beauty speaks for itself, needing no elaboration, so I shall not attempt to elaborate on this many faceted passage. I leave the words on the next page to speak for themselves – I have the rest of my life to attempt to respond to this particular challenge!

Ann Bird

With every person who dies, part of us is already in eternity. We must, if we love this person, live up to the great encounter of a living soul with a living God. We must let go of everything that was small, that was separation, alienation and estrangement, and reach out to that serenity and greatness, newness and abundance of life into which the departed person has entered. We should not speak of our love in the past tense. Love is a thing that does not fade in a faithful heart. It does not go into the past unless we betray our love. We must keep our love alive in a new situation, but as actively and creatively, and more so, more often, than when the person was with us. Our love cannot be dead because a person has died. If that is true, our life must be a continuation of theirs, with all its significance. We must reflect on all that was beauty, and nobility, in that person, and make sure those around us, and our surroundings, do not lose anything through the death. This applies to all families and friends as well as the immediate bereaved, so that the seed that has fallen into corruption may give a hundredfold harvest in the hearts and lives of others.

One thing is at the front, with every bereaved person – the sense of separation, of being left alone. One has to accept it creatively and to say 'I have a double task to fulfil – the dead person's work and my own. I must be great for two, reveal integrity for two.'

* * * *

If I could penetrate the dark dividing us
– I on this side of death, and you on that –
Where should I find you? You must surely be . . .
Where flowers vibrate with colours yet unknown,
Beyond the spectrum of our rainbow arch,
And bird-song has a meaning now half-guessed . . .
Where love and joy are almost tangible . . .
It is all there – and here, and everywhere,
Had we but eyes to see Reality.
If you came back you would confirm it all.

Muriel Grainger

LET YOUR GOD LOVE YOU

Be silent.
Be still.
Alone. Empty
Before your God
Say nothing.
Ask nothing.
Be silent.
Be still.
Let your God
Look upon you.
That is all.
He knows.
He understands.
He loves you with
An enormous love.
He only wants to
Look upon you
With His Love.
Quiet
Still.
Be.

Let your God –
Love you.

Edwina Gateley

Creator of rainbows,
come through the closed doors
    of our emotions, mind and imagination;
come alongside us as we walk,
come to us at work and worship,
come to our meetings and councils,
come and call us by name,
call us to pilgrimage.

Wounded healer,
out of our dis-unity
may we be re-membered,
out of pain of our division
may we see your glory.
Call us from present
pre-occupation
to future community.

Spirit of Unity,
challenge our preconceptions,
enable us to grow in love and understanding,
accompany us on our journey together,
that we may go out with confidence
into your world as a new creation –
one body in you,
that the world may believe.

Kate McIlhagga

PAIN,
PREJUDICE,
POWER AND
POSSIBILITY

1. PAIN

Didst thou not make us one,
That we might one remain,
Together travel on,
And share our joy and pain,
Till all thy utmost goodness prove,
And rise renewed in perfect love?

Charles Wesley

What a marvellous, truth-filled hymn this is and how easy it is to sing it in the company of those of like mind and attitude with a lovely cosy feeling that all will be well with us, and that even the pain of which this verse speaks probably won't be too bad! But we all know deep down that it is not going to be the case and that the vast majority of us can only cope with the pain that life inflicts upon us as we journey together if we can share it with others in depth and with safety.

A friend suffering from acute physical pain told me that she had been visited by a well-meaning member of her church who talked about everything other than the one thing about which she needed to talk – the pain that was gripping her. 'At that point,' she said, 'I was incapable of getting beyond the pain – each moment of coping was a little victory for me – and the need to share so that I was not alone in it all was overwhelming.'

When we are in severe pain, whether it be physical or emotional, we feel alone with ourselves. Everything contracts into the centre of our pain so that things which normally support us and cushion us in our everyday experience seem to lose their permanence and reliability, and our independence, security and confidence are easily threatened.

In such circumstances we all – even the strongest of us – need to 'borrow' strength from others. We need not only those who will be with us and care for us but those who will listen to our fears, our anger and our doubts and who will be with us in the silences. The Psalmist's recognition of the need for the healing resource of companionship and for dependence on strength other than one's own is clearly reflected in his words, 'Even though I walk through the darkest valley, I fear no evil; for you are with me . . .' And as God enters into our situation of pain with us so, too, we often find him through the ministry of those who share the pain alongside us.

Physical pain, such as my friend was enduring, can be excruciating. Although modern medicine is able to give relief in many situations, even with analgesics and pain-killing injections pain is never easily borne unless there are those close by prepared to do all in their power to enter into the pain as much as possible. There are two telling examples in a book about coping with pain – a woman, speaking of her husband's presence with her in hospital: 'When I get home I won't be able to tell the family what the pain was like, but he will.' And a patient at home: 'Even if I have my eyes closed because the pain is so bad I know she is there and that helps me hold on . . .'

Carl Rogers, the psychologist, defines this kind of warm creative relationship as 'sensing the other person's private world as if it were your own, but without ever losing the "as if" quality. We have to try both to empathise in this way to the greatest possible extent and to remain apart enough to have our own strength to offer as support and comfort.' In Morris West's *The Clowns of God* there is a moving example of such a relationship. Jean Marie, the exiled Pope, is visiting his friend Carl Mendelius who lies desperately ill in hospital after the explosion of a letter-bomb:

> 'Carl, this is Jean. Can you hear me?' There was an answering pressure against his palm and more helpless gurgling as Mendelius tried in vain to articulate. 'Please don't try to talk. We don't need words, you and I. Just lie quiet and hold my hand. I will pray for both of us.' He said no words. He made no ritual gestures. He simply sat by the bed clasping Mendelius' hand between his own, so that it was as if they were one organism: the whole and the maimed, the blind and the seeing man. He closed his eyes, and opened his mind, a vessel ready for the inpouring of the Spirit, a channel by which it might infuse itself into the conjoined consciousness of Carl Mendelius.

The result of that pastoral visit was that 'there was a calm so powerful that he could feel the fevered pulse of the sick man subside like sea waves after a storm'.

As we stay beside our relatives, our friends and those who need our love in situations of physical pain of differing intensity we have to risk being hurt and wounded ourselves as we struggle to take the pain and brokenness of another person into our own consciousness. It is a hard and costly ministry that is required of us. The disciples in Gethsemane found it too hard – they fell asleep. But if we can 'stay there and stay awake' we shall not only be helping to lessen the isolation felt by the one who is in pain, we shall also help them to see their pain in terms of meaning and significance.

Personal physical pain is only one aspect of the terrible pain that afflicts our world. The pain which men and women inflict upon each other in the name of the causes they espouse or as a result of their prejudices, and the hatred that consumes them, is indescribable. We have only to look at the TV pictures of the fighting in particular trouble spots or read of the communities starving to death because of the greed and indifference of others, to be reminded of this on a daily basis.

As we try to take some tiny fraction of such pain into ourselves on their behalf we should have no option but to offer our strength and influence to change their situation in terms of political pressures, money, sharing of technology – whatever can, to a greater or lesser extent, alleviate the agony of such unnecessary desperate suffering. Much of our own pain pales into insignificance in the face of such horror. But even then we cannot afford to remain with our eyes focused only on distant places when communities much closer to us and individuals within them are crying out for our understanding and care as they attempt to live full lives while hampered by their own particular isolating and demoralising pain.

This pain can take so many forms. For example, although the pain of loneliness is borne bravely by an immense number of people, for others it becomes a disabling state which mars all their relationships and separates them from everything human which most of us take for granted. The pain caused by change or by disadvantage can be deeply scarring, and the pain which we inflict upon each other through our prejudice is the ground for a great deal of our hurting.

Certainly it would be true for all of us that we cannot live in relationships with others without knowing pain. In fact the more joy our relationships give the more possibility they create for pain – the pain of separation, of misunderstanding, or of alienation. On the other hand, the more we love each other the more sensitive we become to each other's pain and the more we long to alleviate it whenever possible.

C S Lewis said:

> God whispers to us in our pleasures,
> Speaks in our conscience,
> But shouts in our pain.
> It is his megaphone to rouse a deaf world.

Many of us would recognise the truth of this. If we have been able to confront our own pain honestly and creatively we have known the hand and heart of God within our devastation. Sadly, though, so often those whose pain is greatest do not have either the knowledge or the means to project their needs with sufficient clarity to reach those who could best alleviate their pain. And even if they do we, who are supposed to be God's listeners in this world, put our hands over our ears and shut out the cries of pain because to hear them would demand too much of us in terms of time and energy and loving involvement.

Unfortunately for us, those words of Charles Wesley's hymn that might at first have seemed to us a comfortable sharing for the select few are nothing less than the costliest of all demands; to recognise and live by the fact that as human beings we are all members one of another and we can never be free from each other's pain any more than we should stand back from each other's joy.

Ann Bird

I believe, although everything
hides you from my faith.
I believe, although everything shouts No! to me . . .
I believe, although everything may seem to die.
I believe, although I no longer would wish to live,
because I have founded my life
on a sincere word,
on the word of a Friend,
on the word of God.

I believe, although I feel alone in pain.
I believe, although I see people hating.
I believe, although I see children weep,
because I have learnt with certainty
that he comes to meet us
in the hardest hours,
with his love and his light.
I believe, but increase my faith.

Livre de Cantos

* * * *

Healing power of Jesus Christ,
fall afresh on me,
Healing power of Jesus Christ,
fall afresh on me.
Touch me, stir me, enfold me, love me.
Healing power of Jesus Christ,
fall afresh on me.

Howard Booth

2. PREJUDICE

All that kills abundant living
Let it from the earth be banned;
Pride of status, race or schooling,
Dogmas that obscure your plan.
In our common quest for justice
May we hallow life's brief span.

Fred Kaan

Nothing had really mattered, the teaching, the talking, the example, the patience, the worry. It was all as nothing. They, like the strangers on buses and trains, saw only the skins, never the people in those skins. Seales was born among them, grew up among them, played with them; his mother was white, British, of their stock and background and beginnings.

All the hackneyed clichés hammered in my head. A coloured boy with a white mother, a West Indian boy with an English mother. Always the same. Never an English boy with a West Indian father. No, that would be placing the emphasis on his Englishness, his identification with them.

It was like a disease, and these children whom I loved without caring about *their* skins or *their* backgrounds, they were tainted with the hateful virus which attacked their vision, distorting everything that was not white or English.

This extract from *To Sir, With Love* by E R Braithwaite was written several years ago, but, to our deep shame, black and Asian people living in the United Kingdom today would testify that little appears to have changed. In the excellent study pack entitled 'One Race' published by the Churches' Commission for Racial Justice, example after example is cited of occasions when black people have been mindlessly attacked, when abuse has been hurled with no provocation and when discrimination and prejudice are still viciously present.

Those of us who do not live in multi-racial, multi-faith areas must never be guilty of making glib statements about the pain and outrage of those who have to live on the receiving end of the indignities and frustrations with which black people and those of minority faiths have to contend. Neither must we assume that this is not our problem and ignore the possibility that our own black friends and acquaintances, or those whose lives touch ours briefly in shops or at work or in hospital, may not always find themselves entirely at ease in our company.

We can all be thoughtless and unkind at the best of times and if we are unprepared to acknowledge the endemic power of racism for all of us we are likely to add to the woundedness and marginalisation of those we most want to affirm. We can only, wherever it is appropriate, listen and learn and care and try to change public perception and behaviour in any way in our power.

But racism is not the only evil prejudice in our society. We all begin life's journey from very differing places and it is obvious that the culture from which we come, the home in which we grow up – or the lack of it – and the security or otherwise of our relationships will all have a lasting influence on our future judgements and ideas about others.

From an early age we are conditioned by pressures and assumptions which are quite beyond our control. If I am born into a Moslem family I am likely to grow up as an adherent of the Moslem faith. If I am nurtured within a family that worships within the conservative evangelical Christian tradition, that is likely to be the church background in which I feel most comfortable. If my parents have no particular beliefs I may well view what convinced believers in the God of any faith have to say as out of date and irrelevant; and if I come from a background where I am surrounded by those who are prejudiced against anyone who is markedly 'different' from me, I am likely to have to change my own attitude quite radically as I begin to think and judge for myself if I am to shed the prejudices and indoctrination of my youth.

Where I think we often fail each other as Christians and as members of the wider social community is that we don't allow for the difficulty and struggle of mind and heart such change of attitude can involve. We tend to assume that we are all at the same stage in conquering prejudice and we do not see the need to talk with people about the genuine difficulties they have with certain attitudes and beliefs.

Someone, for example, may feel scarcely any racial prejudice but have a real problem with the issue of homosexuality. Another person may have no time for anyone who comes from a wealthy home background but will do everything in their power to persuade people to use inclusive language. To make matters more complicated, we are prone to believe that we ourselves are free from prejudice and thereby fail to recognise how deeply ingrained our presuppositions are about people whose ways and customs are not ours.

It is true that in recent years issues such as racism, sexuality, disability and sexism have all been high on the Church's agenda, and not before time. Yet is is no use our supposing that the deep pain and hurt caused over centuries by the arrogance and lack of care of any particular section of the community in regard to another is going to disappear in a decade or so. Added to which we know, if we are honest about it, that much of the prejudice and fear still exists.

Fear of the unknown, fear of 'difference' is a very powerful factor in our lives and I do not believe any one of us is immune from its crippling influence, however much we may protest our liberal and radical views. We all, whoever we are, and wherever we are coming from, have 'hang-ups' in some direction. The way we were taught history in schools, the effects of living near difficult neighbours, even a chance remark we overheard as a child – all sorts of haphazard happenings influence how we think and how we react, and we all need to have the courage to look with honesty and clarity at how we really behave towards others.

My plea is that we shall allow ourselves to be open enough in the company of those we trust to share what our true feelings are about any particular prejudice we have. Then we can help and encourage each other to move forward to a deeper understanding of our common humanity and the basic need of every man, woman and child to be accepted for who they are and to be accorded the dignity and just treatment that God intends for every individual.

What we can never afford to do is to be complacent. To 'speak the truth in love' to each other and to listen in love in response is only of value if we do so with the rigorous intention of eliminating prejudice not only within ourselves but also in every area of life that our influence can touch. And our lack of prejudice must never be simply skin-deep. It is so easy to think that one lacks prejudice and still to be patronising and shallow in the face of other people's deeply wounding hurt, rejection and anger. In the words of Ralph Wright:

We are so clumsy with the pain
of other people
we – so full of comfort so content
to toss our velvet coated words
like crusts to beggars – fail to diagnose
the nausea men feel for trite maxims.

Our prejudices must be brought into our prayers in the knowledge
that to do so will prove costly and will demand of us conversion and
repentance and a humble willingness to learn new attitudes and truths.
One thing we know for sure is that God is not prejudiced. His
indiscriminate love accepts each one of us and loves each one of us. The
only label he puts on each one of us is the seal of his blessing and his
unfailing care.

Ann Bird

* * * *

God, we praise you for your love in Christ,
challenging all our definitions,
overturning all our stereotypes.

Wondering, amazed, in Christ we see you:
        the king of the universe, washing dirty feet;
        the creator of heaven and earth, hungry, cold and tired;
        the saviour and healer, wounded with the pain of the world
        the almighty lord, found with the weak and vulnerable.

God, help us to be strong in the love and liberty of Christ
so that we can follow the same pattern of service:
        with the inner security that frees us
            from the drive to seek reward or recognition;
        with the confidence to give those whom we serve
            the dignity of voicing their own needs;
        with the patience that does not try to impose your will
            or our own,
        but works and waits for your justice.

In the name of Christ,
Amen.

Jan Berry

Beatitudes . . . for friends of people with disabilities

Blessed are you who take time to listen to difficult speech,
  for you help us to know that if we
  persevere we can be understood.

Blessed are you who walk with us in public places and ignore
the stares of strangers
  for in your companionship we find havens
  of relaxation.

Blessed are you who never bid us to 'hurry up', and more
blessed you who do not snatch our tasks from us,
  for often we need time rather than help.

Blessed are you who stand beside us when we enter new and
untried adventures,
  for our failures will be outweighed by the
  times when we surprise ourselves and you.

Blessed are you who ask for our help,
  for our greatest need is to be needed.

Blessed are you who help us with the graciousness of Christ
who do not bruise the reed nor quench the flax,
  for often we need the help we cannot ask for.

Blessed are you when, by all these things,
you assure us that the thing that makes us
individuals is not in our peculiar muscles,
nor in our wounded nervous system, but in the
God-given self that no infirmity can confine.

Rejoice and be exceedingly glad, and know
that you give us reassurance that could never
be spoken in words, for you deal with us as
God has dealt with all his children.

Anon

* * * *

O Lord our God, you know who we are; people with good consciences and with bad, persons who are content and those who are discontented, the certain and the uncertain, Christians by conviction and Christians by convention, those who believe and those who half believe, those who disbelieve.

And you know where we have come from: from the circle of relatives, acquaintances and friends, or from the greatest loneliness; from a life of quiet prosperity, or from manifold confusion and distress; from family relationships that are well ordered or from those disordered, or under stress; from the inner circle of the Christian community or from its outer edge.

But now we all stand before you, in all our differences, yet alike in that we are all in the wrong with you and with one another, that we must all one day die, that we would be lost without your grace, but also in that your grace is promised and made available to us all in your dear Son, Jesus Christ.

Karl Barth

* * * *

O God, whose longing is to reconcile the whole universe inside your love, pour out your abundant mercy on your Church, and on your world so fragmented and torn apart.

For the long history of pain and travail, of oppression and prejudice inflicted on women and men, within the Church and in the world,

O God forgive us and pour out your mercy.

For our failure to be open and responsive to the possibility of new freedom and new hopes,

O God forgive us and pour out your mercy.

For our failure to resist the bitterness which poisons and sours the gospel of love and reconciliation,

O God forgive us and pour out your mercy.

For our failure to present a wounded world with hope for reconcilation in a true and loving community of women and men,

O God forgive us and pour out your mercy.

O God, whose longing is to reconcile the whole universe inside your love, pour out your abundant mercy on your Church and your world so fragmented and torn apart; this we plead through the love of Jesus Christ which already surrounds us.

Source unknown

3. POWER

On those who fight on earth for right relations
We pray the light of love from hour to hour.
Grant wisdom to the leaders of the nations,
The gift of carefulness to those in power.

Fred Kaan

Power, in human terms, is not something with which the Methodist Church appears to be comfortable. 'Mission Alongside the Poor', mission alongside the marginalised and the under-privileged is at the top of our priorities and that is absolutely as it should be. And yet we cannot actually achieve anything in the way of change and improvement in society without having recourse to power in some form or another. After all, the point about the poor – in whatever context that word may be appropriate at any given time – is that they are powerless. Therefore our longing is to make it possible for circumstances to change in such a way that all who feel powerless are able to take enough power to themselves to have the possibility of choice and freedom for themselves. Therefore we try to do everything in our own power to work for a world where all can enjoy human dignity and mutual respect and freedom to choose, knowing that, in the end, justice can never be separated from considerations of power.

What kind of power, then, do we have within the church to overturn existing systems and attitudes and economic orders? And do we not only use that power effectively but also support the people who are trying to use such power for good sufficiently? There is, of course, the personal power possessed by each one of us who does have choice, comparative freedom and a comfortable lifestyle; the Gospel is a continual challenge to us in relation to our use of money and possessions and time. It is a challenge to us also not to allow pride or apparent self-sufficiency to cloud our judgement in such a way that we do not recognise our spiritual poverty and our need for God's grace and forgiveness.

On the other hand, choice also brings opportunity and power properly used enables us to contribute towards change for good. Our own personal discipline and our efforts to use what power or influence we may have to work at the economic and political consequences of our faith are not alternatives. This is where sometimes the church's attitude to those who wield such power saddens me. We give glad support and affirmation to those who work in deprived areas, who care for the sick,

152

who are involved in mission enterprises in the inner city. We are far more ambivalent towards those who hold positions of responsibility in multi-national companies or who work in banking or industry or local government. Yet these men and women, who worship with us Sunday by Sunday, are at the centre of the places where crucial decisions are made, where moral issues are not clear cut because they are so complex and where the implementation of policy has such far-reaching effects that even with the best of intentions, fatally wrong decisions can be made.

Such people carry a very heavy load on our behalf. In a world where profit and success are rated of paramount importance it can be excruciatingly lonely if one is trying to live and work and influence decisions by different standards. Added to which, the power that brings responsibility and gives authority over others also exacts its own price. For example, I have many friends with whom I worship who have agonised over having to make others redundant and who have needed great pastoral support themselves in that situation as they in turn try to be pastorally concerned for the individuals involved. 'To do justly, to love mercy and to walk humbly with one's God' is not an easy option in the world of power.

So although in many ways it is a great privilege to have at least some opportunity to change the face of one's own immediate little world – or indeed that of the much wider world – we are all human and we all need each other's support and understanding. And that does not always seem to be readily forthcoming in today's Church environment. Prejudices all too often exist against those who are powerful, are comfortably off or – perhaps worst of all – who live in suburbia! This is so sad. Mockery and indifference can often wear down our faith more effectively than outright hostility. As Solzhenitsyn reminds us: 'The line separating good and evil passes not through states or between classes, nor between political parties . . . but right through every human heart and through all human hearts.'

No one of us is perfect. Not one of us does all he or she could to redress the imbalances in an imperfect world. Most of us in the church are trying to struggle with the issues involved and to act accordingly. But we are far less likely to attempt to change ourselves or the world around us if we are constantly disabled by a sense of guilt which is being fostered by other people. God uses us where we are and as we are – he alone is our judge. If, in our openness to him, we are called into new situations or provoked into adjusting our priorities, that is a different matter, but we have no right to impose guilt on each other.

It is not easy for the powerful and the rich to enter the kingdom of heaven and yet . . . Jesus himself spent a great deal of time in Capernaum, one of the most well-to-do places in the Israel of his day, and he enjoyed the hospitality offered in the home of Martha and Mary. The rich Joseph of Arimathea was one of his accepted followers. Although there was nothing sentimental or simplistic about his attitude it seems that Jesus' judgement on the powerful and the comfortably off was not nearly as harsh as is the judgement of many to people in similar situations today.

As Christian Aid's Michael Taylor reminds us: 'He doesn't have time for outsiders, but no time for insiders. He will eat and drink with insiders as well, though he refuses to kow-tow to them and conform to their manners and standards of behaviour. And he doesn't look at outsiders through rose-coloured spectacles. He doesn't share the romantic view that all the poor and all the sinned against are entirely virtuous. Some are morally at fault. Many are not. All are sinners just like the rest of us, but none of that justifies their exclusion. And if they're not allowed in, then he will go out – outside the boundaries of the social camping ground – and exclude himself with them.'

There is a fascinating passage in Evelyn Waugh's novel about Helena, the mother of Constantine, where Helena meditates on the three kings who came to worship at Bethlehem:

'How laboriously you came, taking sights and calculating, where the shepherds had run barefoot! How odd you looked on the road, attended by what outlandish liveries, laden with such preposterous gifts! . . . Yet you came, and were not turned away. You, too, found room before the manger, your gifts were not needed, but they were accepted and put carefully by, for they were bought with love. In that new order of charity that had just come to life, there was room for you, too. You were not lower in the eyes of the Holy Family than the ox or the ass.'

Helena then prays for all those with different kinds of riches:

> 'All who are confused with knowledge and speculation, of all who through politeness make themselves partners in guilt, of all who stand in danger by reason of their talents. For his sake who did not reject your curious gifts, pray always for all the learned, the oblique, the delicate. Let them not be quite forgotten at the throne of God when the simple come into their kingdom.'

There is a great danger that we unthinkingly allow prejudices within the fellowship of the church to cripple our outreach in a totally unnecessary fashion. In ecumenical gatherings we hear much talk of 'the pain of our divisions' and rightly so, for anything that separates and wounds the whole Body of Christ is a scandal and negation of the Gospel we preach. But it is also a scandal if we do not need to look as far as the ecumenical scene to perceive such divisions. We shall become more powerless to 'turn the world upside down' if we cannot be accepting of one another within the church.

Whether we live in suburbia, in the inner city or in a country village; whether we vote for one political party or another; whether we prefer to worship in one tradition or another; we are all loved and accepted by God. We are who we are for a multiplicity of reasons. Our backgrounds, personalities, relationships – so many things – condition us and mould us. We do not fully understand our own insecurities and fears or motivation and needs. We can never afford to be judgemental of each other. That is a sure way to deprive each other of power.

On the other hand we can give each other power. We can encourage and enable one another and recognise each other's gifts. We can have time for one another. We can respect each other's opinions and value each other's unique contribution within the mission of the Church as a whole. We can, in fact, empower all around us if we see *all* people as children of God and as part of his loved creation. In this way we shall live in the power of love and on a wider scale we shall also begin to understand the truth expressed by Ralph Waldo Trine in this extract from *In Tune with the Infinite*:

> 'There is only one religion. Whatever road I take joins the highway that leads to Thee,' says the inspired writer in the Persian scriptures.

> 'Broad is the carpet that God has spread and beautiful are the colours he has given it.'

'The pure man respects every form of faith,' says the Buddhist. 'My doctrine makes no difference between high and low, rich and poor; like the sky, it has room for all and like the water, it washes all alike.' 'The broad-minded see the truth in different religions, the narrow-minded see only the difference,' says the Chinese. The Hindu has said, 'The narrow-minded ask, "Is this man a stranger or is he of our tribe?" But to those in whom love dwells, the whole world is but one family.'

Ann Bird

* * * *

For this reason I bow my knees before the Father, from whom every family in heaven and on earth takes its name. I pray that, according to the riches of his glory, he may grant that you may be strengthened in your inner being with power through his Spirit, and that Christ may dwell in your hearts through faith, as you are being rooted and grounded in love. I pray that you may have the power to comprehend, with all the saints, what is the breadth and length and height and depth, and to know the love of Christ that surpasses knowledge, so that you may be filled with all the fullness of God.

Now to him who by the power at work within us is able to accomplish abundantly far more than all we can ask or imagine, to him be glory in the church and in Christ Jesus to all generations, forever and ever. Amen.

Ephesians 3:14-21

Power Games

When we play God
We throw our weight around,
Treat people like chess pieces,
Play our game regardless of their
Gifts. Their value lies in
Cost-effectiveness, not in
Intrinsic worth. And if we lose,
We simply change the rules
And use them to our own advantage.

Lord, it must sometimes
Break your heart, to see how
We mismanage your creation,
Misuse freedom. Are you sometimes
Tempted to break our teeth,
Hurl thunderbolts, cry
Halt?

It must be most
Frustrating
Being
God.

Ann Lewin

Father, source of all power, we confess that we do not always use the powers you have given us as you intend. Sometimes we are afraid of the power we wield, and so do not use it at all; at other times we are careless in our use of it and harm others; at yet other times we deliberately misuse it to achieve our own selfish ends. We confess our misuse of our God-given powers, and ask for your grace to use them properly in the future.

We think of the power of the nations of the world. In international affairs it so often seems that events are out of our control, and rule us. Father, help us to see how national power can be wielded for the fulfilment of your will.

We think of the power of economic systems. Often we feel enmeshed in a system which is not fair and yet cannot be changed without causing immense hardship. Father, help us to become masters of economic forces and to order them for the purposes of justice.

We think of the power of governments. They now touch our personal lives at so many points. Father, may politicians and civil servants use their powers responsibly and respect the rights of individuals.

Give us the courage to challenge them when they are wrong, and willingness to share in the processes of government ourselves. May the power of governments everywhere be used for the good of all.

Father, yours is the ultimate power. We see evidence of it everywhere in the world, but most of all in Jesus Christ. In him we see the power of your love: weakness and death did not destroy him and you raised him from death. May that same power of love be in us.

Caryl Micklem

* * * *

Make us keep the sputtering lantern burning
and not to break a wounded reed.
Make us understand
the secret of eternal life
from the pulse of blood in our veins
and realize the worth of life
from the movement of a warm heart.
Make us not discriminate
the rich and the poor
the high and the low
the learned and the ignorant
those we know well and those we do not know.
Oh!
A human life can't be exchanged for the whole world,
this supreme task of keeping the lives
of sons and daughters of God.
Let us realize how lovely it is
to feel the burdens of responsibility.

A worker of Peace Market, Korea

4. POSSIBILITY

Great God, your love has called us here,
as we, by love for love were made.
Your living likeness still we bear,
though marred, dishonoured, disobeyed.
    We come, with all our heart and mind
    your call to hear, your love to find.

We come with self-inflicted pains
of broken trust and chosen wrong,
half-free, half-bound by inner chains,
by social forces swept along,
    by powers and systems close confined,
    yet seeking hope for humankind.

Great God, in Christ you call our name
and then receive us as your own,
not through some merit, right or claim,
but by your gracious love alone.
    We strain to glimpse your mercy-seat
    and find you kneeling at our feet.

Then take the towel, and break the bread,
and humble us, and call us friends.
Suffer and serve till all are fed,
and show how grandly love intends
    to work till all creation sings,
    to fill all worlds, to crown all things.

Great God, in Christ you set us free
your life to live, your joy to share.
Give us your Spirit's liberty
to turn from guilt and dull despair
    and offer all that faith can do
    while love is making all things new.

Brian Wren's hymn says it all. His words sum up everything that lies at the heart of our caring ministry. Called by a loving God to share his love gladly and indiscriminately we find him ministering with us and to us in all our pastoral concerns and needs. In his offer of freedom and hope for all people, including ourselves, we discover – if we dare to have eyes to see – the endless possibilities for new life and fresh beginnings that can transform so much that could be considered purely negative, destructive and hurtful.

Yet we all know that it is so much easier to affirm this in words than to live in its spirit! And what is true of us as individuals is all too often true of the Church in its historic and global context. The contradictions between our preaching and our practice have meant that where we have preached liberation we have often practised oppression, where we have preached peace we have frequently fought against each other, and where we have preached about the bias to the poor we have, in the West, become increasingly rich at their expense. We have allowed difference of race and class and domination by the few to be accepted norms in society and we have affirmed God's created world in relation primarily to our own immediate pleasure and need while paying scant attention to urgent environmental issues.

And on a more personal level we do not always show God's gracious love to each other. We are often judgemental and suspicious of one another and indifferent to each other's needs, preferring to protect ourselves from people and situations that make us uncomfortable because if we really looked at each other with love and if we really 'called each other friends' it might prove too costly.

Yet there is a better way and it is a way that is open to us all. One of my special memories is of the christening of my granddaughter, Jane. It was a very special service not just because it was a lovely, happy family occasion but because in his sermon the minister, Charles New, encouraged us to embrace the kind of Christian life that I believe God intends for us all. His hope for Jane, and for the rest of us, was that we should discover within our Christian discipleship 'enjoyment', 'flexibility' and 'optimism' – and I came away from the church aware that the more I thought about those themes the more power to heal and challenge and renew I found within them.

I will not attempt to reflect on the words as Charles did, but I am grateful to him for the fact that he made 'enjoyment' his starting point because to do so underlines the positive, creative, welcoming attitude God invites us to offer to each other in all our personal relationships and in our social and political activities.

To enjoy people is to see the best in them, to accept them as they are and to appreciate their courage and their unique value. It is to live our lives in an atmosphere of gratitude for other people's individuality and giftedness. It is to rejoice in their difference from us as well as to delight in our similarities to each other. And it is to encourage and affirm others rather than allowing ourselves to criticise and undermine those who threaten our security or stir up jealous feelings within us.

To enjoy people as God wants us to do is also to enjoy ourselves and our own specialness in his sight. For unless we can value and accept ourselves we shall find it difficult to enjoy and value the relationships we form with other people. Loving is a giving and receiving to and from each other – the enjoyment is in the mutuality.

Nor in our enjoyment of life must we underestimate the power and grace of laughter and perhaps especially of laughter which does not deny the pain and suffering which comes to all of us along the way. In an article in *Contact*, a magazine for counsellors, Lionel Blue wrote:

> The grace of humour should not be underrated – for grace it is. It has helped Jews transform their own bitterness. In Jewish jokes about Hitler, for example, he always comes over as a figure of fun, not as a portent of horror. A great deal of life is tragedy, and suffering is woven into it. A lot of it cannot be changed – it is part and parcel of what we are and the world we live in. The only thing we can change is our attitude to it. The same event can be regarded as tragic, farce, or comic. Judaism assimilates tragedy by refusing to accept it on its own terms . . . We have to protect our souls from our hate and bitterness.

Thelma Bailey, who is a woman with severe physical disabilities, has published two books of poems entitled *With Tongue in Cheek* and *Thank You Lord*. In one of the introductions Thelma writes:

> Thank you Lord – I AM GLAD TO BE ALIVE! Why? Because disabled or not, God has a purpose for every one of his children. Yes, whatever we may look like on the OUTSIDE, it's just as Paul says: ' . . . Some of the parts that seem weakest and least important are really the most necessary. Yes, we are especially glad to have some parts that seem rather odd!' – 1 Cor 12 vv 22-23.

Whether we are sound in mind and body, or whether we rely on other people and machines to enable us to function more effectively, we can ALL respond to God's love for us!

Love is a journey of discovery on which we seek to know God's will for us. On that journey we will be faced, on occasions, by steep, rough roads and enjoy scenic beauty. There are periods of testing and times of refreshment. Always there are fellow travellers and ALWAYS, GOD IS WITH US, just as he promised.

Thelma experiences constant pain and weakness, she will have faced prejudice in terms of her disability and she is not endowed with the kind of power secular society recognises. Yet she radiates the power of love and her faith and hope transcend both pain and prejudice. In spite of all that life has dealt her Thelma enjoys it to the full.

Flexibility might at first glance seem a less demanding attribute, but for some of us it is often particularly difficult. We become set in our ways of thinking and of behaving, and because the majority of us cling to what we see as security we can become very apprehensive of change.

Yet we can only respond fully to others if we are flexible in our attitude and in our willingness to listen to other people's points of view and experience. It is unlikely that we shall be asked to give up all that we hold dear or important, but we are expected to test our certainties, assumptions and prejudices against the measure of God's love and graciousness and to look at people and situations in a clearer perspective for his sake. To do so is not always easy. We all relate to others on his behalf 'half-free' and 'close confined' and he longs to loosen our 'inner chains' so that we can approach life more generously and with a humility that acknowledges we do not have all the answers. To be open to God's will for us will always demand flexibility on our part or we shall find we have set our own agenda ahead of our prayerful attention to him and that is bound to be constricting.

When, however, prayer and expectancy go hand in hand and when we have the courage to trust ourselves to God's loving direction and purpose for us, we shall be able to face the future optimistically even when life is difficult and the changes required of us are costly. In fact we are more likely to discover 'the hope that is in us' when we are able to remain positive and trusting even at the worst moments of life than we are at life's sunniest moments. John Bluck in *Everyday Ecumenism* writes:

> We have to trust the divine significance of what we learn in our crisis and brokenness and failure, in our uncertainty and doubt and despair. When our marriage breaks down or our health packs up, when our financial security crumbles, our career plans collapse, when our five-year programme falters after five months, when our children fail to perform as happy clones who get straight 'A's and always go to church, when we find that our friends think we're smug and superior, or irrelevant and unmeaningful, when our attempt to reach out is rejected, to share is misinterpreted, to explain is heard as defensive – whenever we are left out, left over, edged out to the margin of our middle-class, middle-road existence, there, exactly there and then, do we have the best chance to hear and see and feel and know what God is up to . . .

In the midst of circumstances such as these, when pain is at a premium, when people are prejudiced against us and when we feel at our most powerless, we need to see God's possibilities for us more than ever. In the strength of his love for us we can be truly optimistic in spite of everything.

If in our heart of hearts we want to be 'set free' and to set others free, his love really will 'make all things new' and then, imperfect though we know ourselves to be, we shall be caught up much more completely in offering 'all that faith can do' to take part in God's loving design and to

> Suffer and serve till all are fed,
>   And show how grandly love intends
> To work till all creation sings
> To fill all worlds, to crown all things.

Ann Bird

Come, listen and learn.
Do not judge others and their ways;
instead respect them and love them.
Open your hearts to them.

If you come in this way,
open, listening humbly, without judging,
then gradually you will discover
that you are trusted.
Your heart will be touched.
You will begin to discover the secret of communion.

* * * *

Love is a much maligned word.

Real love is attentive, and concerned for the other person. It respects the person just as he or she is, acknowledging the bad but recognising the potential for growth, however well this may be concealed.

Love believes in the beloved, even when it seems crazy and hopeless, and rejoices in her inner beauty even when nobody else can see it. 'I don't care what they say. It doesn't always have to be like this. I believe in you and I know that you can do great things.'

Love rejoices in the presence of the other person and in the beauty of his or her heart even if it remains quite hidden.

Love creates deep and lasting bonds whatever the setbacks.

All too often we take an interest in someone only when we can 'do good' in order to 'feel good': in which case we are loving ourselves, trying to enhance our own self-image. It is only too easy to love people when it suits us so that we can feel 'useful' or even 'successful'. When they start to disturb us and make increasing demands we put up barriers in order to defend ourselves.

Real love is quite different. It is to forget ourselves sufficiently to allow our hearts to beat at the rhythm of another: it is to suffer alongside; it is compassion.

So, do not shrink from suffering,
but enter into it
and discover there the mystery
of the presence of the risen Jesus.
He is hidden there, in the sacrament of the poor.

And do not turn aside from your own pain,
your anguish and brokenness,
your loneliness and emptiness,
by pretending you are strong.

Go within yourself.
Go down the ladder of your own being
until you discover –
like a seed
buried in the broken, ploughed earth
of your own vulnerability –
the presence of Jesus,
the light shining in the darkness.

And there, offer yourself with Jesus
to the Father
for the life of the world.

* * * *

Today as yesterday
Jesus is calling us to follow him,
to walk in his footsteps.

He is calling you and me to be like him,
wherever and whoever we are,
whatever we think of ourselves.

To live as he lived,
to love as he loved,
to speak as he spoke,
to offer our lives as he offered his,
to do what he did,
to do even greater things
because of his going to the Father.

Jean Vanier

O God of love, we pray thee to give us love:
Love in our thinking, love in our speaking,
Love in our doing, and love in the hidden places of
    our souls;
Love of our neighbours near and far;
Love of our friends, old and new;
Love of those with whom we find it hard to bear,
And love of those who find it hard to bear with us;
Love of those with whom we work,
And love of those with whom we take our ease;
Love in joy, love in sorrow;
Love in life and love in death;
That so at length we may be worthy to dwell with thee,
Who art eternal love.

William Temple

PASTORAL PRAYERS

A blessing from God for visitors/listeners

My child,
Listen to your heart.
You will find there all the emotions
and all the experience you need
to meet with this other soul.
Trust your own heart,
And now, forget it.
Your heart will guide you in your response
without you worrying about it.

Listen to me.
I am your Lord,
And in seeing this person you please me.
I will guide and uphold you in all you say and do.
Trust me; you have made my heart glad
and I will not fail you.
Now forget about me.
I will be with you without you thinking about me.

Listen to this other person.
I am in them whether they acknowledge it
or you see it.
But more even than discovering me in them,
just discover them;
this other human soul
in need of a heart into which to pour their troubles,
for their own heart is soaked through with pain
and can hold no more.

Listen,
and bring refreshment to a heart that cries to speak its
story.

A prayer for visitors who give themselves in hope of being used by God

Lord, I am afraid.
How can I bring relief to this person?
Who am I to think that I can enter into another's
    experience,
and share with true sympathy their burdens and hopes?
There is nothing I can do to substantially change this
person's suffering.

All I can do is go and spend time with them
and expose my inadequacy
and my vulnerability
and hope that somehow they will see a faith and love
that restores to them a hope that they too will know
again
the peace and confidence to live in harmony.

A prayer for standing on the doorstep

Lord, if I should wait to ring this bell until I have a comment, sensible and well thought out, appropriate to the occasion, which will bring the person within comfort and hope, then I shall never ring it, but hesitate with finger poised or walk away defeated. So, give me grace just to ring it and set in train a visit that cannot then be withdrawn, and in the turmoil of this encounter may my desire to bring comfort and hope be taken by you in place of any skill and used by grace through faith to accomplish your purpose in my calling.

Short form

Lord, a fool here rushes in; by grace, may my visit be taken to be that of an angel.

A prayer for visitors desiring to communicate the love of Christ

Lord Jesus Christ,
I want to be you to this other person,
at the same time that I am utterly myself;
in my body to incarnate your love,
in my posture, in every gesture,
in each word I speak and in my silence
to communicate your acceptance and forgiveness;
by the look on my face to express sympathetic understanding;
to radiate strength and hope just by being there;
to give faith and trust that is picked up and used when I leave;
to give courage to face up to truth, even if I am afraid myself;
to encourage the breaking free of all that harms and destroys;
to restore a joyful hope in living;
and to do all this by being me, but being me as I follow you;
being Christ to another; discovering Christ in another,
and sharing our humanity, infused with grace.

A prayer for God's help before meeting with/visiting someone

Lord, I cannot do this by myself. I am not worthy, I am not skilled. I am afraid I will make mistakes; say the wrong thing; put them off by my manner or the look on my face. Yet I want to help this person. I want to meet with them, at a deep level, in the name of Christ, and on behalf of the whole Church. And I hope that somehow, by your grace, because you will be there with us, that our time of sharing will be for the healing of body, mind and soul; for the renewal of relationships; for the springing up of hope and faith; that another person will take a step towards wholeness of life because I gave myself into your hands, and believing myself to be doing your will, for the sake of your Kingdom, have committed myself to this meeting.

A prayer of committal to God of a meeting/visit

Lord, I have done my best. Our meeting seemed to me to be all right, but did I really touch home – or allow myself to be touched? Success and failure are hard to assess and sometimes very deceptive. Can I leave this meeting in your hands, with my prayer that you will use my presence, my listening, my words, my silence, my wisdom, my confusion, all to relieve the suffering of the one with whom I met. I wholeheartedly desire that they should find relief and I believe that you are the source of their hope.

A prayer to say to yourself when in trouble in the midst of an encounter

Lord, calm and direct me; help me to give myself to this other, and to be a channel of your grace. Set them (him/her) free to find new life; and give me now either the words or the silence that will lead us on a path from here, to wholeness.

A prayer for visitors/listeners who want to care for the other person

Lord,
you care.
This I believe with all my heart.
Teach me to care,
for this is what I want.

I desire so to love others
that I will seek their wholeness
with all my will,
and every gift that you have given me.
By your grace at work in me
may I wrestle at understanding
till I strike a spark of sympathy,
and sink deep into your love
till I well up with compassion,
and act, to make your gift of healing real.
Give me discernment to decide and persevere,
so that my sharing in your care
may bring home to others your care for them,
and quicken them to join in the fellowship of your love.

A prayer for a suffering person – which a visitor could also pray on their behalf – expressing God's care for all people, and his leading of them to wholeness.

Lord,
I ask for your silent touch
to reach my wound
and give me hope of healing.

Be sensitive to my frailty
for I have come face to face with my own mortality
and it frightens me to think that I shall cease to be,
unless there is indeed life in you.

I want to know that I am included in your care,
and called to fellowship with the human race.
So, by your presence, reassure me of my worth
and by reaching out, and being reached toward, make contact.

May my tears not fill the pool of my despair,
but be for the cleansing of my soul
and the refreshment of my spirit of wholeness,
watering the roots of all that is good and pure and lovely.

Though I drift or founder, hold my hand to the rudder
and command me to still take charge of my pain,
for, as much as I know I need help, any solution must be my own
expressing the person I am, and holding the seeds of the person I am
called to be.

And be not too gentle with me.
Give me courage to hear your word
till my brokenness is mended into your image
and all your fullness of life begins to open up in me.

Transform me as I meet with Jesus.
With nothing to say, let me listen to his compassion.
Be hard or soft as I need, for you always set free.
Set my feet on the path to salvation till I know I already have it.

Tender mercy, renew me.
Overflowing love, caress me.
Grace, strong enough to bear all my sorrows and failings, uphold me.
Hope, never-failing, put laughter in my heart, and I shall face the day.

I ask that repentance will give me energy to change;
that I will take your forgiveness to my heart and let it warm me through.
Lift up my head to discover on some horizon a banner of meaning
and, taking up all my experience, I offer my whole self to love as you love me.

A blessing of God's confidence in us

> Beloved,
> You have all the gifts you need;
> I know, because I gave them to you.
> You have skill and insight,
> experience and care.
> You have faith and love to move mountains –
> as small as a mustard seed, I mean, but that is enough.
> So, go, and be my ambassador.

Denis Vernon

Acknowledgements

Page

2, 56, 137   Edwina Gateley, 'Called to Become', 'The Sharing', and 'Let your God love you', Anthony Clarke, Wheathampstead, Hertfordshire and Source Books, Ca. Trabuco Canyon, California.

7, 94   Kate Compston, 'Dear God, teach us to see people', and 'Seeing with Love' © Kate Compston 1987, from *Encounters*, the Prayer Handbook for 1988, published by the United Reformed Church in the United Kingdom.

9, 96   Jean Vanier, *The Broken Body*, Darton, Longman and Todd.

10   Julie M. Hulme, from *The Light Beyond the Wall*

26   Francis Brienan, 'Christ, you are calling' © Francis Brienan 1994, from *A Restless Hope*, the Prayer Handbook for 1995 published by the United Reformed Church in the United Kingdom.

32   Harper Lee, *To Kill a Mockingbird*, Pan Books.

38   Kenneth G. Phifer, 'I Need to Listen' from *A Book of Uncommon Prayer* Copyright © 1981, by Kenneth G. Phifer. Used by permission of The Upper Room.

39   Listening and Reflecting drawing reproduced by permission of the Scripture Union.

48   Michel Quoist, 'The Telephone' from *Prayers of Life*, Gill & Macmillan.

68, 81   Fred Pratt Green from 'When the Church of Jesus' (*Hymns & Songs* 74) and from 'God is here! As we his people' (*Hymns & Psalms* 653), Stainer & Bell Limited.

99, 145, 152   Fred Kaan, from 'For the healing of the nations' (*Hymns & Psalms* 402) and from 'We turn to you, O God of every nation' (*Hymns & Psalms* 412) Stainer & Bell Limited.

101   Allan Boesak, *Walking on Thorns – The Call to Christian Obedience* © 1984 WCC Publications, World Council of Churches, Geneva, Switzerland.

102   Oscar Romero, *The Violence of Love – the words of Oscar Romero*, HarperCollins.

104   Joe Seremane, 'You asked for my hands', Christian Aid/SPCK.

104   Michael Ramsey, 'Most merciful Father', from *The Book of Christian Prayer*, SPCK.

107   Wallace Stevens, from 'Six Significant Landscapes VI', *The Collected Works of Wallace Stevens*, Faber & Faber Limited.

109   (Cartoon) Stuart Matthews and Ken Lawson, *Caring for God's People*, St Andrew Press.

109   Tim Hansel, *When I Relax I Feel Guilty*, David C. Cook Publishing Company, available from Nova Marketing, UK distributors, Eastbourne.

110-111   Lionel Blue, 'A Holiday from Myself' from *Bolts from the Blue*, Hodder & Stoughton.

112   Michael Hollings and Etta Gullick, *You Must be Joking, Lord* © McCrimmon Publishing Company Ltd.

Page

'Caring Matters', 'Tracing the Rainbow' and 'Pain, Prejudice, Power and Possibility' orginally appeared as articles in the *Methodist Recorder*.

Line drawings in 'Focusing In' by Frances Biseker.

Stained glass window photograph by Arthur Creighton.

Called To Care

A Pastoral Handbook

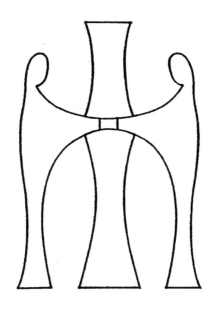

Edited by
Ann Bird

Called to Care
A Pastoral Handbook
Edited by Ann Bird

© The Methodist Church

ISBN 1 85852 074 6